Purposeful Play with Your Preschooler

A Learning-Based Activity Book

14

Purposeful Play with Your Preschooler

A Learning-Based Activity Book

Anthony C. Maffei, Ph.D.
and
Teresa M. Hauck

With a Foreword by
Patricia Buckley, M.A.

INSIGHT BOOKS

Plenum Press • New York and London

Library of Congress Cataloging-in-Publication Data

Maffei, Anthony C.
    Purposeful play with your preschooler : a learning-based activity
book / Anthony C. Maffei and Teresa M. Hauck ; with a foreword by
Patricia Buckley.
        p.   cm.
    Includes bibliographical references (p.) and index.
    ISBN 0-306-44325-2
    1. Early childhood education--United States.   I. Hauck, Teresa M.
II. Title.
LB1139.25.M34   1992
372.21'0973--dc20
                                                        92-20896
                                                            CIP

ISBN 0-306-44325-2

© 1992 Plenum Press, New York
A Division of Plenum Publishing Corporation
233 Spring Street, New York, N.Y. 10013

An Insight Book

Printed in the United States of America

With love to our families—

To Doris, James, Tom, Ashley, Lesley, and Kim

—ACM

To Ed and Melissa

—TMH

Foreword

This book is intended for adults involved with preschool children. If born now, these youngsters will enter the work force during the early part of the twenty-first century, 2010 to 2020. Would anyone be foolhardy enough to predict the skills that will be necessary for gainful employment during this time or even a future time—a time whose dates look even stranger to us? We can no longer teach children rote solutions to routine problems since we cannot even venture to guess what the problems will be 20, 30, or 40 years from now. But one skill is absolutely certain: *each child must develop his or her ability to think to the optimum of his or her potential.*

How can caring adults foster this development? Certainly, it would help us to understand the stages of child development so that the time spent with our children is enjoyable, both for the adults who see the child's face light up as he gains new knowledge and the youngster who views the activities as interesting rather than frustrating experiences.

Someone said that time is money and, like money, time is something none of us has enough of. The activities suggested in this book will help you make the most of the time you spend with your child. Don't waste the precious early stages of your child's development drilling the youngster in unnecessary or incorrect skills. Don't waste those minutes in tasks inappropriate to the age and ability of your child. This book will show you how to make these times happy and productive.

PATRICIA BUCKLEY

Butler, NJ

Acknowledgments

Many bodies of work, as in the case of a book, a piece of music, or a painting, have their start as an idea which then goes through the long journey leading to a completed product. Potentially good ideas sometimes remain abstractions, for they fail to gain the necessary support from a variety of people. Without key people who gave us inspiration, made comments, and offered encouragement, this book would still be just that—an abstraction.

Consequently, we would like to first recognize Norma Fox, our contact person and Executive Editor at Insight Books, for guiding and shaping our idea into its proper form. Also, Patricia Buckley, now a retired college professor and fellow author, not only let us use the math activities from her *Teaching Preschool: Foundations and Activities* in Part II of our book, but also critiqued our work. Her words of wisdom and years of experience are also reflected in the Foreword. Yvette Pond and Bridget Lockett put their creative minds and talented hands to work and produced all of the professional-looking drawings in the book and on the front cover. Carol Adams gave us help and suggestions for turning our individual drafts into a clearly and correctly written whole. Doris Barlow Maffei, mother of five, provided the ideas that formed the outline for Part II.

Kathy Douglas not only provided wonderful ideas for activities in Part II but, as a friend and assistant to Teresa M. Hauck, gave much support and encouragement. Thanks also go to Edward Hauck and Francine P. McQuaide Obrero for contributing the adorable photographs and to the children and adults in them. Shucilah Kalliappan, Mary June "MiMi" and Jim "Paw Paw" Hauck, Kim Griffiths, and Jennifer and Amie Whipple were wonderful assistants for caring for and entertaining Melissa, the daughter of Teresa M. Hauck, while Mommy was working on this book. Thanks to Melanie "Pete" Norris, Joni Kelly, Karol Rockey, Jim Hauck, and Velma McQuaide for contributing an activity to Part II, as well as to Aissatou "Mama" Bah and Bridget Lynch for each of their activities and also caring for and enteraining Melissa. Dr. Nancy Kimmons, Director for Family Life Services at Florida State University, gave support and encouragement as did Alison Iglehart of Tallahassee Community College. Thanks to our spouses, Doris and Ed, for their patience, understanding, encouragement, and ideas; without them we would never have completed our task.

Jean Piaget (1896–1980) must be mentioned as one of the first to elaborate on theories of how children acquire knowledge. Without him there would be no idea. Anthony C. Maffei was first introduced to Piaget many years ago when he was a graduate student in mathematics education, studying with Jack M. Ott at the University of South Carolina. Then later, while teaching the mathematical applications of Piaget's theory to future preschool teachers, Anthony developed an idea that culminated in the above-mentioned book written with Pat. Norma also contributed to that idea when she was editor of Human Sciences Press (now part of Plenum). About four years ago, that same book led to another idea that eventually developed into the work before you now. It is hoped this book will be of value to all those who are fortunate enough to be involved in the excitement and joy of watching and participating in the learning process with preschoolers.

Finally, thanks to the following who have given us permission to quote from their books:

Excerpts from *The Essential Piaget,* edited by H. Gruber and J. Voneche. Copyright © 1977 by Basic Books, a division of HarperCollins Publishers. Reprinted by permission of the publisher.

Piaget, Jean, and Inhelder, Barbel. *The Psychology of the Child.* Translated from the French by Helen Weaver. New York: Basic Books, 1969.

Pulaski, Mary Ann Spencer. *Understanding Piaget.* New York: Harper & Row, 1971.

Pulaski, Mary Ann Spencer. *Your Baby's Mind and How It Grows.* New York: Harper & Row, 1978.

A. C. M.
T. M. H.

Contents

I • FOUNDATIONS

II • ACTIVITIES

APPENDIXES

Part I

FOUNDATIONS

Chapter 1

Introduction

SURVIVING

A generation ago, families usually survived on only one income while the mother raised the offspring. Today's cost of living, along with the gradual emergence of women into traditionally male-dominated fields, has changed this. Many women today want a career before beginning a family. Consequently, the mother's age at the birth of her first child has shifted, to some degree, to a mother who is usually college-educated, has a successful career, and is somewhere between her late twenties and middle thirties. For those who can manage it, a small number of women have even decided to put their careers on hold for a while and stay at home to raise their children during these crucial early years. However, statistics show that the trend is that more mothers are entering the work force.

A GROWING TREND

The last decade of the twentieth century, when compared with the decade before it, continues to show a growing trend in the number of mothers entering the work force.

The 1980s saw the passing of a watershed: 51% of the mothers of infants returned to work before their child's first birthday. That figure quickly became history. By 1989, 52% of the mothers of infants were employed. By 1995, we expect two-thirds of the mothers of preschoolers and three-fourths of the mothers of school-age children to be in the labor force.[1]

The increasing number of mothers in the work force has also raised some concerns about the care that is given to the children. Both parents, but especially the mother, must first come to grips with the pressures that are placed on the family unit when, for a good part of the day, one or both parents are on the road, in a plane, or at the office, and someone else is watching the children.

Eventually, many parents realize that their preschoolers would probably benefit from the experience of socializing with their peers in a situation where doing and making are the activities of chief concern. However, a serious problem develops when parents relinquish most of their quality time with their preschooler to a day-care "family." The typical excuse for relinquishing time is the inability to find the time in the evenings when everyone is just too exhausted or on weekends when neglected errands have to be done, not to mention the single-parent family, where finding the time is an even more difficult task.

When parents must leave their young ones in local or company-owned day-care programs, the need to be with their children does not diminish. When children are picked up at the end of the day, parents need to leave their work frustrations at the office and get involved with their children. The task of nurturing is a parental responsibility that should not be relegated to parental substitutes. The purpose of this book is to make parental involvement easier during the times when parents and children are together.

THE PRESCHOOL YEARS

Research tells us that the preschool years play an important role in the future lives of children in terms of learning intervention and parental involvement. For our purposes, we will say that the 1- to 5-year-old age group makes up the preschool age, the preformal school years. Parents realize that a significant event happens in the lives of their children when they are 2 years old. The children begin to think, as reflected by speech. Prior to this stage, children think internally and use gestures to indicate what they want. If they are hungry, they may lead a parent by the hand to the refrigerator.

The emergence of speech means that the child is capable of comprehension and insight. First-time parents are usually amazed and overjoyed that they can finally communicate with their offspring. Grandiose plans for the child's future emerge. This pride is both natural and normal for parents. When most children are 2 years old, their logical development begins to emerge, and parents need to nurture it. However, parents must take care that they provide an atmosphere for their children that is within the range of the child's developmental abilities.

STRUCTURE VERSUS UNSTRUCTURED

How do parents talk with their preschoolers? What can they say other than "no" when their child misbehaves? Do parents read to the child often, have her read back, let him do simple math problems, or have her discuss her day? At the preschool age, a child obviously cannot carry on a two-way conversation with any degree of maturity. We shall discuss the reasons for this inability later.

Some parents get distraught because their child cannot do some basic math, read, or follow simple directions. As a result, they get anxious and overprepare children with activities that will only lead to more frustration for both child and parents. Parents are wasting their time when they take this approach, but most of all they are missing out on the fun and enjoyment of learning with their child.

Parents, however, should not give up and resign themselves to watching TV during most of their quality time with their children. Surely there will always be enough of this passive medium for everyone. Conscientious parents need to be actively involved in the development of their preschoolers, employing those activities that will help them in their later formal-learning years while at the same time developing an emotional bond with them.

ABOUT THIS BOOK

This book is important for any parent who desires to spend the time he has available with his preschooler in a meaningful manner. Part I discusses the child's cognitive ability, considering how young children acquire knowledge and what reasons inhibit typical preschoolers from usually following a line of reasoning and why activities involving "let's pretend" and "make-believe" are more effective in reaching out to them.

Part II contains activities that will explore the many ways parents and their children can enjoy each other. It offers interesting, creative, but mostly simple things to do in places where today's hurried parents and their children are often found together: in the store, at the park, at home, or in the car.

The need for parents to spend time with their preschoolers is crucial. This beginning relationship is the basis from which future relationships will evolve. Sound preschool–parent relationships will form the foundation for solid preadolescent–parent relationships, which, in turn, will plant the same seed for the adolescent period. When the child becomes an adult, he will value these associations and realize the need for continuing the same with his children.

No doubt those parents who would use this book have already thought about creating a bond with their child that will grow as the family grows. Finding the time to help children learn and think will enable them to develop feelings of self-worth and self-esteem and will help produce well-adjusted adults.

Chapter 2

Beginning Intellectual Development

INTRODUCTION

Jean Piaget (1896–1980) was a Swiss psychologist, educator, and author of over thirty volumes. His major contribution was in the field of beginning intelligence. Through his keen observational skills of young children, he showed how emerging intelligence goes through various stages of intellectual development as we interact with others and the environment. As an educator, he believed that students should be involved in the process of inventing and discovering their knowledge rather than being told what and how to do things.

According to Piaget, our intellectual as well as physical development is based on our ability as biological organisms to adapt to our environment. Adaptation means adjusting to the environment in order to meet our needs. For example, through the process of evolution certain animals have grown fur to adjust to a changing climate. Infants learn not to touch things that are hot. Adaptation, then, involves two interrelated ideas: *assimilation* and *accommodation*.

ASSIMILATION AND ACCOMMODATION

In a cognitive sense, assimilation is the process by which we are actively involved in absorbing anything around us, such as ideas, ob-

7

jects, events, and so forth. A 1-year-old assimilates things by putting anything and everything within his reach into his mouth. From these experiences he will accommodate or learn what he likes and dislikes. The process of accommodation will also allow him to determine what is harmful and must be avoided:

> The processes of assimilation and accommodation are in balance. The infant attempts both to modify his behavior in response to the demands of the environment (accommodation) and to understand this environment in terms of his own schemes (assimilation).[1]

Both assimilation (absorbing) and accommodation (adjusting) to the environment involve an active, conscious process by which we seek a balance, or what Piaget calls "equilibration."

FACTORS AFFECTING THE BALANCE

The process of maintaining equilibration in assimilating and accommodating to the world around us is central to Piaget's theory of how children learn. However, equilibration is affected by several factors, one of which is physical growth, or what Piaget calls "maturation." For example, as an infant's fine muscles grow, so will his ability to learn and do things he was unable to do before. Adjusting to the first-time experience of holding and then scribbling with a crayon brings about an adjustment in the child's equilibration and, consequently, the development of a new learning experience or schema.

Socialization or verbal communication is another factor challenging a young one to learn. This takes the form of information and directions received from peers and parents. Experience is another factor affecting equilibration. Theoretically, if a young one were prevented from exploring (assimilating and accommodating) things in his environment, he could maintain equilibration but show no mental growth. Mental development, for Piaget, is a continuous, dynamic process of adapting and accommodating in which equilibration is disturbed and simple or complex cognitive structures or schemas result. This learning adventure (Fig. 2-1) is marked by certain discernible periods or stages in the mental development of a child.

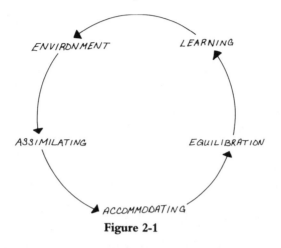

Figure 2-1

FROM BIRTH TO 2 YEARS OLD

The first stage of development, referred to as the sensorimotor period, occurs from birth to about 1 1/2 to 2 years of age. The mental development of the child at this stage is described in terms of sensory (senses) and motor (movement) ability. Six phases make up the sensorimotor period. The time that each phase begins and ends, as well as any of Piaget's stages of intellectual development, are always approximate. Their occurrence depends on the factors that were discussed above: maturation, socialization, and experience. If some children develop physically at a slower rate than other children and their experience of things around them is limited, then their intellectual development will occur at a later age.

Beginning Phases

At birth, an infant exhibits very basic biological movements: sucking, grasping, kicking, and so forth. He is unable to focus his eyes clearly and he has no awareness of things outside the realm of his own consciousness. This phase, called the "reflex stage," lasts for about the first six weeks after birth. Even at this stage, the baby is assimilating and accommodating to the experiences around him, which, for Piaget, marks the beginning of intelligence:

> The baby is born into this world equipped with certain innate, uncoordinated reflexes such as sucking, swallowing, grasping, and crying. Primitive though they may be, these are the building blocks of intelligent behavior. For Piaget the biologist as well as Piaget the psychologist, "intelligence is adaptation."[2]

Employing the observational skills he learned as a biologist observing the adaptive ability of snails and mollusks, Piaget witnessed similar abilities in infants as they adapted their innate reflexes to environmental stimuli.

The next phase, which occurs between the ages of about 6 weeks to 4 or 5 months, involves the development of elementary habits. As the child begins to coordinate his reflexes, new unintentional adaptive schemas of habit are produced, as in the case of the hand and mouth reflex (motor and sucking reflexes):

> The next step is for these two reflexes to be joined, so that when the hand grasps something like a rattle, it is brought to the mouth to be sucked. At first this combination of behaviors takes place without the baby's seeing what it is that he is grasping. Gradually, with much repetition, he learns to coordinate his kinesthetic and motor activities so that he can control the movements of the rattle across his visual field.[3]

The newborn "learns" a new schema as he coordinates two basic reflexes which then emerge as a habit. As infants continue to explore with their bodies, they learn and develop other habits that will stay with them and eventually grow in complexity.

The Middle Phases

The third phase covers the period from approximately 4 to 9 months. Babies begin to break away from their egocentrism and realize that there is a world out there. This marks the beginning of children trying to coordinate some of what they have learned with their environment:

> If you watch your baby you will notice his eager response to each new experience. He may accidentally bang the slats of his crib, or kick a mobile hanging over it, causing it to flutter. Often he will stop quite still and listen or stare; then he may smile at this unexpected phenomenon.[4]

Here children are using their kicking ability to explore other avenues of learning. The fourth phase of the sensorimotor period begins around 9 months and lasts to about 1 year of age. This marks the start of purposeful behavior since children use what they have developed to seek out new ends. For Piaget, it also means the beginning of memory and the appearance of observable intelligent activity.

Piaget often used observations of his children to formulate his theories of intelligence. These findings were later corroborated by other scientists. Observing his daughter, who was 8 months and 20 days old at the time, use an acquired habit to serve a purpose, Piaget states:

> Jacqueline tries to grasp a cigarette case which I present to her. I then slide it between the crossed strings which attach her dolls to the hood. She tries to reach it directly. Not succeeding, she immediately looks for the strings which are not in her hands and of which she only saw the part in which the cigarette case is entangled. She looks in front of her, grasps the strings, pulls and shakes them, etc. The cigarette case then falls and she grasps it.[5]

The Final Phases

The last two phases of the sensorimotor period demonstrate gradually increasing complexity in children's thinking ability. During the fifth phase, which runs from approximately 1 to 1 1/2 years of age, children experiment with new means to reach a desired goal. Their beginning ability at walking also gives them newfound freedom:

> The child wants to know more about objects . . . He begins to stack blocks instead of knocking them down. He fits containers

inside each other, or drops small objects into a tin cup, listening to the difference in sound between a metal ring and a wooden bead.[6]

The last phase of the sensorimotor stage, from about 1 1/2 to 2 years of age, is significant for two reasons. First, it represents the transition to Piaget's next stage of cognitive development, the preoperational stage (2–7 years old). More important, the child now is able to think things out in his mind before testing his ideas in practice. It is the beginning of insight and what Piaget calls representational thought:

> In this stage, the child becomes capable of finding new means not only by external groping but also by internalized combinations that culminate in sudden comprehension or insight. For example, a child confronted by a slightly open matchbox containing a thimble first tries to open the box by physical groping (reaction of the fifth phase) but upon failing, he presents an altogether new reaction: he stops the action and attentively examines the situation . . . after which he suddenly slips his finger into the crack and thus succeeds in opening the box.[7]

Representational thought allows the child to have images in his mind of how things might actually happen. These images, as in the case of the matchbox, represent the physical object. However, as we will see in the next chapter, the thinking of a 2-year-old is rather limited.

Chapter 3

The Years from
Two to Five

FACTORS AFFECTING LOGICAL THINKING

The characteristics of preoperational thinking will be discussed in the next several chapters of Part I and will cover the rest of our major area of interest, namely, the years from 2 to 5. The young preoperational child shows signs of thinking on his own. These mental activities, or "operations," as Piaget refers to them, are not logical (in fact, they are prelogical!) and are restricted to how things look and appear.

Also, the speech that children begin to use around 8 to 12 months of age, during the sensorimotor period, is actually imitative speech. Sounds are mostly repeated, as in the case of the precious and famous "da da" and "ma ma," and reflect things and people around the child. In comparison, the single most important characteristic of the pre-operational period is the emergence of language, which frees the child's thought processes from dependence on objects, people, and movement, thus enabling him to go through daily experiences at a faster rate than before.

The topic of language will be looked at later. For now, we turn our attention to how the thinking of 2- through 5-year-old children affects their ability to reason. There are at least six distinct but related factors that limit the preoperational child's ability to reason and think logically:

1. Egocentrism
2. States
3. Transductive reasoning
4. Centrations
5. Irreversibility
6. Animism

Parents, caregivers, and educators should recognize these factors as part of the child's natural development.

Egocentrism

Egocentric behavior means that the child's thinking is self-centered. This type of behavior is different from the egocentric behavior of adults, although such behavior in adults is usually the exception rather than the rule. For preoperational children, it is the other way around, for they believe that everyone thinks like they do. They consider their thinking as the right thinking and, as a result, never feel that they have to be accountable for their actions.

Piaget believes children's egocentric behavior during the preoperational period has its beginnings in the prior sensorimotor stage in that " . . . with respect to material objects or bodies, the infant started with an egocentric attitude, in which the incorporation into his own activity prevailed over accommodation (remodification of behavior as a result of experience)."[1] The expression "you can't reason with a child" should be an important piece of advice for everyone who must recognize a child's inability, as a result of egocentric behavior, to engage in any type of formal reasoning.

The existence of egocentric thought does not mean that preoperational children cannot learn anything. It does imply, however, that they learn best when the thinking is less abstract and less formal, as in the case of "hands-on" materials such as blocks, beads, rods, and string. Open-ended games such as "let's pretend" and "make-believe" allow a child to express himself freely and do not include many rules to follow.

States

Another factor that limits children's thinking ability is their tendency to focus on the *states* of a given event. This means that they are unable to follow transformations in a sequence, but instead focus only on states or certain aspects of a sequence. For example, an adult holds a crayon in a vertical position on a desk. The adult releases the crayon and it falls onto the desk in a horizontal position (Fig. 3-1). When asked to draw the falling stages of the crayon, the preoperational child tends to draw either the vertical or the horizontal states of the crayon, but fails to conceptualize the falling crayon as undergoing a series of different steps or transformations.

Transductive Reasoning

Another factor limiting the thinking ability of the preschooler is *transductive reasoning*. Transductive reasoning is generally characterized as the child's inability to think inductively or deductively. In the formal operational period (11 to 15 years old)—the last stage in Piaget's theory of cognitive development—adolescents are usually capable of drawing

Figure 3-1

conclusions from observable facts. They are also capable, when given some general rules, of deducing specific facts. The former type of reasoning is called "inductive" and the latter is called "deductive." The preoperational child, on the other hand, can only reason from particular, to particular or transductively.

Piaget observed this type of thinking in his 3-year-old daughter, Lucienne, when she did not want to take her afternoon nap one day. She reasoned that, because she didn't take her afternoon nap, it was not afternoon.

> In this case, Lucienne's thought proceeded from the nap (one particular) to the afternoon (the second particular) and concluded that the afternoon depended on the nap, when of course the relationship was a different type.[2]

Try a similar experiment on your own preschooler and observe the results. For example, tell him that all living things with four legs are called animals and that a lion is a living thing with four legs. Then ask him for some more information about the lion. In all likelihood your child will describe other specific features of the lion, such as his whiskers or his roar, without making the conclusion that the lion is also an animal. Children of this age are unable to reason from a given general statement about animals to the specific fact that the lion is also an animal.

Centration

Centration is another example of the perceptually oriented type of thinking that is characteristic of this age group. Some of us tend to read a book based on its exterior appeal; that is, we "judge a book by its cover." This type of thinking typifies the preoperational child whose cognition is very much dominated by the external characteristics of an object. Such children tend to focus on specific traits or features of objects rather than take into account all the features of the objects. As a result, they are unable to *decenter,* that is, to go beyond the perceptual features of objects and view them as representing a whole. Evidence of preoperational children's inability to decenter can be illustrated by presenting them with two rows of like objects, such as raisins. One row should contain eight raisins and the other six (Fig. 3-2). The row with eight raisins should be shorter than the row with six. If children are then asked to choose the row they would prefer to eat, in most instances they will choose the spread-out row (in our picture, the bottom row) because it appears to have more. They are unable to rationally stand back and weigh the situation from the perspective of amount.

Irreversibility

Some of the features inherent in centration can also be seen in children's inability to transform (states). These features can also be seen in children's inability to reverse their thinking. The idea of *irreversibility* versus *reversibility* is a key concept according to Piaget. Reversibility essentially marks the difference in thinking between the preoperational and the next period of intellectual development, the concrete operational stage, which covers the period when children are around 7 to 11 years of age.

Preoperational children cannot reverse their thinking because of their fixation on the perceptual aspects of objects. Concrete operational children, on the other hand, are capable of reversing their thinking and consequently are not limited in their reasoning by the appearances of things. An example of irreversible thinking occurs when the preoperational child pours water from a test tube into a glass (Fig. 3-3). He firmly believes that the amount in the glass is less than the amount that

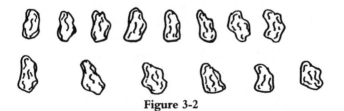

Figure 3-2

Figure 3-3

was in the test tube. The child is unable to realize that the quantity of water is the same in both containers, regardless of their shapes. His centering on a particular perceptual aspect of the experiment, namely, the length of the test tube, inhibits his ability to think logically.

Children in this stage of development are also unable to follow a line of thought back to its beginning point. Their thinking, which has its origins in the sensorimotor period, is irreversible.

> Preoperational thought retains much of the rigidity of sensorimotor thought even while surpassing it in quality. It is slow, plodding, inflexible, and dominated by perceptions. As such it remains irreversible. The attainment of reversible operations is extremely difficult for the child. This is reasonable if one considers that all sensorimotor operations are irreversible by definition. Once a motor act is committed, it cannot be reversed.[3]

Other examples of the preoperational child's inability to reverse thinking are evident in the famous conservation experiments of Piaget, discussed in Chapter 4.

Animism

Egocentric reasoning also produces a related type of thinking on the part of children called *animism*. Since they believe everyone thinks the way they do, preoperational children also believe that the things around them, such as their toys, the sun, and the trees, are real and alive. It's very natural, therefore, to observe them having a conversation with their dolls or teddy bears. Animistic behavior covers a wide age range, from the first stage where anything may be "endowed with purpose and conscious activity" to the last stage where "only plants and animals are considered alive (about 11 or 12 years of age)."

> Objects which move, such as floating clouds or a moving car, are alive. Their movements may be determined by physical compulsion or moral necessity; for example—the clouds "know they must move because they bring rain."[4]

Chapter 4

Additional Limitations to Reasoning

BACKGROUND

Another major area where preoperational children are not ready to reason logically is their inability to conserve. Piaget divides the intellectual development of young children and adolescents into four general periods:

1. The sensorimotor period, 0–2 years old
2. The preoperational period, 2–7 years old
3. The period of concrete operations, 7–11 years old
4. The period of formal operations, 11–15 years old

According to Piaget, these periods of development must be sequential for normal intellectual development to occur. Provided that a child matures at his normal rate, he must encounter enough learning experiences within each developmental period to proceed to the next. Since the ages for each developmental period are approximate, it is quite possible, for example, to find some 8- and 9-year-old children reasoning on the preoperational level.

One of the critical factors that distinguishes the preoperational period from the concrete operational period is the ability of the child to reverse his thinking, as we saw in the case with the glass and test tube experiment in Chapter 3. Unlike children exhibiting preoperational thinking, children who can follow a line of reasoning from its beginning to its conclusion and then back again to the beginning are thinking on the concrete operational level. That is, they are able to reverse their thinking. However, children who think on a concrete operational level are also dependent on material things ("concrete") with which to do their thinking.

SOME IMPLICATIONS

Knowledge of how preoperational children think is helpful to those who design strategies for teaching and for devising appropriate materials for these children. According to Piaget, since thinking ability develops before language ability, activities that emphasize language development over thinking development may be stressing memory over understanding. This means that preschoolers must be given the opportunity to experience new ideas before they learn them by rote. For example, they should understand how to count numbers instead of simply memorizing them. They should spend less time memorizing new words and more time working on activities within the context of the natural language readiness and development of the child. As we will see in Part II, such a curriculum should include simple-to-follow games and activities that will discourage a child from mentally wandering off.

On the other hand, concrete operational thinking is different from formal operational thinking because the latter enables children to reason abstractly without the need to experience things directly. They are able to draw conclusions and make deductions based on the form ("formal aspects") of an argument.

A sound school curriculum for the concrete operational period (usually grades 2–6) should employ a number of hands-on materials since these are compatible with the child's developmental ability. Although Piaget stresses the continuing need to stay in touch with hands-on learning at all grade levels, we will find that many school curriculums, from grades seven on, are less experiment- and project-oriented than they should be. Unfortunately, coupling formal learning that relies mainly on the printed word with direct learning experiences is not always employed in our schools.

There are several different types of conservation experiments that may be used by educators to separate preoperational-thinking children from concrete operational children. These experiments range in complexity from one employing length (usually given to ages 6 and 7) to a task dealing with volume (given to ages 11 and 12). Preoperational children are not developmentally ready to respond to the volume experiments correctly because they cannot reverse their thought processes and they are not able to decenter.

NUMBER AND LENGTH EXPERIMENTS

Conservation tasks dealing with length and number are the standard experiments given to determine whether a child is moving away from the preoperational stage and into the concrete operation. In the "conservation of length" task, a child is presented with two strips of paper of equivalent length. He is then asked to find out for himself if these strips are of the same length (Fig. 4-1). He usually does this by placing them next to each other and comparing the lengths. The experimenter then moves one strip slightly ahead of the other and asks the child if both strips are now of the same length (Fig. 4-2). The preoperational thinker invariably says "no" and points, after being asked, to what appears to be the "longer" piece.

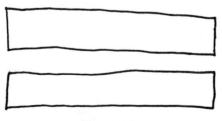

Figure 4-1

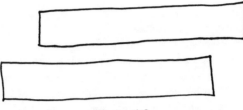

Figure 4-2

In the "conservation of number" problem, two rows of identical objects (here large white buttons), each having the same number, are presented to the child (Fig. 4-3). After the child determines by a one-to-one comparison that each row has the same number of buttons, the lower row is spread out (Fig. 4-4). The child is then asked if both rows have the same number. Once again, preoperational thinkers will point to the spread-out row as having more.

In conservation tasks, the goal is to determine "whether the child can hold constant the quality being considered (conserved) in the face of the transformation. This requires that the child recognize a correspondence between the original form and the transformed one."[1]

CONCLUSIONS

One important result of these conservation tasks deals with the idea of number. A preschooler has not developed a formal understand-

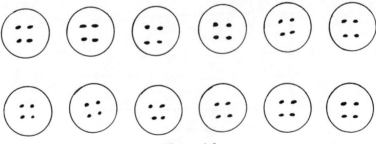

Figure 4-3

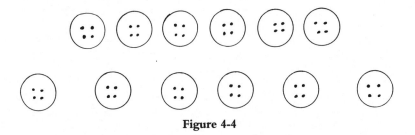

Figure 4-4

ing of number and the reversible operation involved in such an understanding. Conservation tasks are difficult for preoperational children because they are, at this point, unable to distinguish "the forest from the trees" and only focus on the features of an operation. As we shall see later, attaining an idea of number is an essential foundation for understanding an operation such as addition and its reverse—subtraction.

Of course, educators and parents often ask if preschoolers can be taught to conserve length and number so as to prepare them for understanding number at an earlier age. Piaget believes that the child's ability to conserve should come naturally and should not be rushed by teaching, and that only after children have passed through the obstacles to logical thinking at a normal pace will they be ready to start conserving length and number. Research also shows that teaching conservation experiments to preschool children has no real effect on their later mathematical ability or on their ability to remember these experiments at a later time.[2]

Chapter 5

Language and Thinking

INTRODUCTION

An important characteristic marking the preoperational period is the emergence of language. Speaking allows children facility in communicating with others, thus providing a form of expression that up to this point had not been available to them. In the sensorimotor period, children limit their intellectual or thinking ability to their use of objects. If they want to make an idea known to a parent or playmate, they have to do it by pointing to objects or by taking the person by the hand to show them what they mean.

Although the child is already forming ideas in the sensorimotor period, prior to language acquisition these thoughts are different from the logical thinking employed in the later preoperational and concrete periods.

> Intelligence actually appears well before language, that is to say, well before internal thought, which presupposes the use of verbal signs (internalized language). It is an entirely practical intelligence based on the manipulation of objects; in place of words and concepts it uses percepts and movements organized to "action" schemata.[1]

The "action schemata" of the sensorimotor period implies that if we removed a child's favorite toy from his view, it would no longer exist in his mind, and he would naturally not refer to it. However, the development of language in the beginning preoperational years, coupled with a parallel development in thinking ability, now allows a child to form a representation of an object in his mind without relying on the presence of that object. The difference between preoperational and sensorimotor thinking is that the preoperational child can now think about things without having them within sight.

Preoperational verbal behavior, when compared to sensorimotor thinking, improves the range and rapidity of thinking in several ways. Since

> sensorimotor patterns are obliged to follow events without being able to exceed the speed of the action, verbal patterns, by means of narration and evocation, can represent a long chain of actions very rapidly. Sensorimotor adaptations are limited to immediate space and time, whereas language enables thought to range over vast stretches of time and space, liberating it from the immediate. Whereas the sensorimotor intelligence proceeds by means of successive acts, step by step, thought, particularly through language, can represent simultaneously all the elements of an organized structure.[2]

Although the acquisition of language during the preoperational period means that children can begin to express themselves and communicate, their communicating is actually in a unique form. Initial verbal behavior of the preoperational child involves communication with himself or what Piaget calls "egocentric speech." Egocentric speech takes place during the preschool ages of 2 to approximately 5. Later preoperational verbal behavior is characterized as socialized speech and involves communication with others.

EGOCENTRIC SPEECH

Parents, educators, and caregivers should be aware of the characteristics of egocentric speech and adapt themselves accordingly. Such verbal behavior should not be changed or altered; it must be recognized as a natural part of the child's intellectual development and as something that will disappear as the child gets older. Essentially, egocentric speech can be described as a dialogue that a child has with himself.[3] It is usually heard during playtime, which occupies a large part of the child's time. Piaget divides egocentric speech into three categories: repetition, monologue, and collective monologue.

Repetition and Monologue

Repetitive speech is usually most evident in nursery rhymes and favorite songs. Children enjoy repeating words and sentences, not for understanding or communicating, but for the sake of playing with the rhymes and songs or the words and sentences. Repetitive speech has its origins in the sensorimotor period where "in the first years of his life, a child loves to repeat the words he hears, to imitate syllables and sounds, even those of which he hardly understands the meaning."[4]

Another type of egocentric speech that does not involve any form of communicating is the monologue. Unlike repetition, in the monologue the child does carry on a conversation. However, his conversation is not directed to anyone because it is a conversation the child carries on with himself. For Piaget, the origins of monologue are based on the belief that the words of a child are more closely related to his actions and movements than they would be for an adult:

> The child is impelled, even when he is alone, to speak as he acts, to accompany his movements with a play of shouts and words. If the child talks even when he is alone as an accompaniment to his action, he can reverse the process and use words to bring about what the action of itself is powerless to do.[5]

It is very common to find a 3- or 4-year-old, when alone, talking and playing at the same time. Speaking in monologue style allows the child to create a reality that otherwise would be impossible to bring about.

Collective Monologue

The last type of egocentric speech is called the "collective monologue." This type of speech occurs when a child talks aloud to himself with others present. As with the other types of egocentric language, the collective monologue is usually heard during playtime. Early preoperational children make no attempt to communicate with their peers as in the following example recorded by Piaget of children at play:

> Mlle. L. tells a group of children that owls cannot see by the day.
> LEV: "Well, I know quite well that it can't."
> LEV (at a table where a group is at work): "I've already done 'moon' so I'll have to change it."
> Lev picks up some barley-sugar crumbs. "I say, I've got a lovely pile of eyeglasses."
> LEV: "I say, I've got a gun to kill him with. I say, I am the captain on horseback. I say, I've got a horse and a gun as well."[6]

Piaget describes this type of monologue as "the paradox of those conversations between children . . . when an outsider is always associated with the action or thought of the moment, but is expected neither to attend nor to understand."[7] Although it seems that Lev is communicating with someone, the someone is really himself.

TOWARD "GIVE-AND-TAKE"

When children reach the age of 6 or 7, their verbal behavior becomes more social, as indicated by an interest in and concern for what their friends are doing and saying. Although socialized speech cannot be equated with the intellectual "give-and-take" that adults go through, it does include an exchange of ideas in the form of critical remarks, commands, requests, and threats.

Such cooperative behavior of the later preoperational period can be seen in children's games where "following the rules" has a lot to do with winning and losing. This is one reason why games for 3-, 4-, and 5-year-old children should be less structured and more open-ended than games for 6- or 7-year-olds. Early-age preoperational children are not very much concerned with following rules and cooperating with their peers in order to win. At first glance, it would appear that there is some concerted effort to follow the game rules, but eventually a child will usually

> . . . play either by himself without bothering to find playfellows,
> or with others, but without trying to win, and therefore without
> attempting to unify the different ways of playing. In other words,
> children in this stage, even when they are playing together, play
> each one "on his own" (everyone can win at once) and without
> regard for any codification of rules.[8]

The inability of the egocentric preoperational child to communicate with others has considerable impact on his ability to think logically.
Such a limitation will also dictate what and how much he can learn. We
will investigate a suitable curriculum in Part II of this book.

Chapter 6

The Concept of Number

INTRODUCTION

Our next area of investigation is a look at how preschoolers develop the concept of number. Depending on who you ask, the concept of number could have several interpretations. For the teacher, it might mean a student's ability to do well in math. For the scientist, it might mean someone with a natural tendency to reason abstractly with numerals and symbols. But for Piaget, who researched the topic, the answer ties into his theory of cognitive development. Piaget claims that the concept of number has its origins in the development of certain schema that begin to take root during the early preoperational years (and even before that in the sensorimotor period!) and culminate with the child's ability to conserve quantity (or number).

When a child, around the ages of 6 or 7, is able to conserve number, he is usually ready to perform the first basic, related operations of addition and subtraction. That is, he has all the necessary schema in place to understand how addition and its opposite operation, subtraction, are related. For example, the statement "2 + 3 = ?" is an addition problem. The sum is "5." This same problem can be rewritten as subtraction by leaving out one of the addends (the "2" or "3") and by including the sum ("5"): "2 + ? = 5." This problem can also be written in a more common form as "5 − 2 = ?" In both problems the missing addend is "3."

Adding involves combining while subtracting means separating. A child who is able to understand how adding is related to subtracting is able to reverse his thinking and see how subtracting is related to addition. These related operations should be taught in school over a period of time by first introducing actual physical objects to represent the numerals and symbols (for example, combining three apples and five strawberries, as in Fig. 6-1), then pictures to represent the numerals and symbols, and finally the operation in both numeral and symbol (Fig. 6-2) form.

Students who have problems understanding how adding is related to subtracting might not have been provided with enough prior experience and, consequently, do not have the necessary cognitive schema in place. As we shall see, these schema are classifying, ordering, and counting, along with the ability to understand counting and the equivalence of two sets.

CLASSIFYING

Classifying, or sorting, involves the ability to notice the likenesses and differences between a set of objects according to certain properties such as shape, size, or color. For example, a 4-year-old can classify triangles by color and separate the blue and red ones into two piles.

The ability to classify, as well as order, actually begins when children are very young. Long before they are able to classify by the above

Figure 6-1

Figure 6-2

properties, children will notice relationships among things they see, feel, or taste.

> Between the ages of 6–8 and 18–24 months, which is well before the acquisition of language, we find a number of behavior patterns which are suggestive both of classifications and seriation. A child may be given a familiar object: immediately he recognizes its possible uses; the object is assimilated to the habitual schemata of rocking, shaking, striking, throwing to the ground, etc. If the object is completely new to him, he may apply a number of familiar schemata in succession, as if he is trying to understand the nature of the strange object by determining whether it is for rocking, or for rattling, or rubbing, etc.[1]

Parents can help develop this natural ability by giving their children hands-on activities that first will enable them to sort based on a common property such as color, shape, or size. Later, sorting can be done according to two properties such as color and shape: all red triangles here and all blue circles there (Fig. 6-3).

When preschool children are able to discriminate between two things, they are at the same time learning that these objects can also differ in size.

ORDERING

Like classification, ordering develops early in the life of the child. At a very early age, children are naturally capable of ordering three objects that differ, to a degree, in size:

> As early as one year of age, or as the child is moving into the sensorimotor level, he can order by size three objects such as

Figure 6-3

bricks if the size differences are easy to recognize, thus solving the
problem on a perceptual level.[2]

However, preschool children in the age group of 3 to 5 years are unable
to order ten sticks of varying size. In the early stages they take a global
approach to the task, failing to see the actual size difference between
each stick (Fig. 6-4). As they move closer to age 5, children can order
the sticks on a trial-and-error basis but do not always get them properly

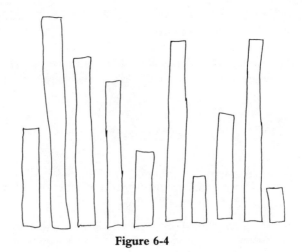

Figure 6-4

aligned (Fig. 6-5). It is not until they are 6 or 7 years old, at about the time when they are able to conserve number, that they are able to draw a mental representation of how the sticks should look and then go about ordering them successfully.

COUNTING AND EQUIVALENCE OF SETS

In the process of sorting and ordering sets of objects, preoperational children are also developing a concurrent schema that is preparing them to compare each set by counting. Counting consists of two basic types: oral and rational. Oral counting means counting aloud to a certain number such as 10, 25, or 100. Parents are naturally impressed with their child's ability to count by rote. This ability, although important, is a less complex skill than rational counting, which asks the question, "How many?" The ability to tell how many elements are in a given pile involves the concept of transitivity: the realization that two sets that are in a one-to-one correspondence have the same number (Fig. 6-6).

Piaget determined that there were three stages of development leading to the development of rational counting. The first stage usually

Figure 6-5

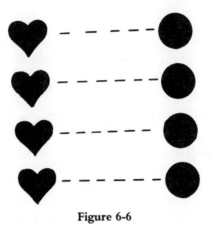

Figure 6-6

occurs around the age of 4. Children at this stage normally do not have a precise notion of cardinal number, that is, the number of elements in a given set when given two sets to compare. Try this exercise by asking your 4-year-old to match two sets by equating the number of objects in each set. Record the results. In a similar experiment, Piaget observed while working with a young child that the child focused on the size and shape of the elements in each set rather than on the number of objects:

> To find the required number of counters to correspond to a collection of 15 elements, he took small handfuls of them and tried to arrange them so that they looked the same: "Are they the same?" "No" "Why?"—"There are more here" (the collection he had just made did in fact contain two extra elements). "Well then? (He did not remove any of the counters, but moved the ones that were too close together, so as to produce a configuration more like that of the model). Is there the same number of counters?"— "No, yes, I've the same amount."[3]

A 4-year-old will say that the above sets have the same number of objects because their shapes are the same. Hence, children tend to make global comparisons based on appearances rather than quantitative comparisons based on a one-to-one correspondence between the elements of each set.

Stage 2 children, who are close in age to 6, are able to make a one-to-one correspondence between two sets of objects only if the two sets are identical in appearance. Altering the size or shape of objects will affect the response as Piaget observed himself when working with a child named Ha:

> Ha first looked carefully at the pile of 15 counters, then put down 16 elements one at a time, copying the configuration of the model bit by bit, looking to see that he was making the correspondence (his one error being due to the fact that he counted one element twice): "Are they the same?" "That one (copy) is bigger. I'll take some away" (removing the extra counter). "Are they the same?" "Yes" "Are you sure?" (the elements of the model were then spaced rather further apart). "Is there the same number of counters?" "Yes . . . no" (he added some counters to the model in order to imitate the new configuration of the copy).[4]

Although Stage 2 children make intuitive correspondence based on appearance, Stage 3 children are fully operational in their thinking. They will intentionally take sets of different sizes and shapes apart to make a one-to-one correspondence. Children who can count rationally usually start doing so around the ages of 5 through 7 as seen in the following example of a 5 1/2-year-old working with two different sets:

> He separated the elements of the model, arranged them 2 by 2 in two vertical rows, then did the same with the counters of his own set, but placed these horizontally. He then saw at once that there was one missing and he added it.[5]

Children who can recognize the equivalence of corresponding sets are ready to conserve number and perform addition and subtraction problems. They have developed a concept of number and have also arrived at the third stage in Piaget's theory of intellectual development: the concrete–operational-thinking period. The concrete operational stage, which we have already discussed, takes place between the ages of 7 to 11 years of age. Chapter 7, the last chapter in our discussion of how children acquire knowledge and develop intellectually, will deal with how they conceive space and time.

Chapter 7

Space and Time

SPACE

The earliest physical experiences of very young children are spatial (geometric) rather than arithmetic.

> Long before children become aware that there are "many" beads on the playpen, they notice that they can push them together, spread them apart. They learn that a ball will roll before they can count three balls.[1]

The child's first impression of the world in which he moves and perceives is a nonrigid one. Topological relationships involving proximity, separation, order, and enclosure (Fig. 7-1) are perceived instead of the rigid Euclidean figures involving circles, rectangles, and squares. Yet it is not uncommon to find parents and educators first helping their preschoolers learn about the properties of triangles, rectangles, and squares. This learning, however, should come after children have been introduced to activities that develop basic topological ideas such as inside, outside, and between.

Piaget notes that at 2 years of age children can first recognize familiar objects, but have difficulty in matching Euclidean shapes:

> Cri recognizes a ball, a pencil, a key, a second pencil, scissors . . . But he cannot identify a cardboard circle from a collection of models, nor draw it. For the ellipse, semicircle with or without notches, the reaction is the same.[2]

41

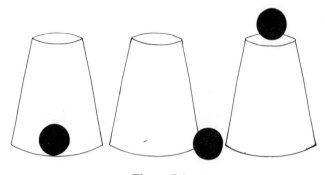

Figure 7-1

Piaget believes that children at this stage of development fixate or center on one aspect of an object. As we have seen with centering, a pre-schooler will tend to focus on specific traits of an object rather than take all of its features into account. For example, when looking at a square, a preoperational child will tend to focus only on its four corners rather than go beyond the perceptual features of an object (the centering) and look upon the square as representing a complete stage. This tendency results from a general deficiency in perceptual activity.

When children are around 4 to 5 years of age, they enter, according to Piaget, a transitional period:

> [The child] recognizes the circle and is able to draw it, likewise the ellipse (which is drawn slightly elongated). In the drawing of the square, one corner is more or less a right angle, the others shown as curved . . . Triangles, rhombuses, etc., are all lumped together.[3]

At this stage of development, children are very active in the exploration of objects. As a result of an increase in perceptual activity, they probe and explore objects and are not just content to grasp or feel the surface of them without further activity.

When they are around 7 years old, children begin to think oper-ationally in that the child can follow a series of actions back to the beginning, as Piaget says during the observation of one of his subjects:

> Tus draws . . . a six-pointed star; [he] explores the six arms re-
> turning systematically to the center to coordinate them. He draws
> it correctly, checking each arm in turn by going back to the central
> reference point.[4]

Although this type of exploration involves perceptual activity, it
also involves thinking that "consists of grouping the elements perceived
in terms of a general plan, and starting from a fixed point of reference
to which the child can always return."[5] Consequently, equilibrium in
thought is reached through a series of explorations and adaptations.

TIME

The child's first concept of time is related to the notion of duration
and a sequence of events that occur when he is quite young:

> The baby's first temporal experience is probably a vague feeling of
> duration; he may be waiting for his bottle and becoming aware of
> the waiting because he is hungry. Soon he learns that events take
> place in sequence and when Mother comes into the room the
> bottle appears soon afterward.[6]

Piaget noticed that children around 1 year old have a distorted
notion of sequence of events. He observed this in the case of his
nephew, Girard, who was playing with a ball when it rolled under an
armchair.

> Girard sees it, and without some difficulty, takes it out in order to
> resume the game. Then the ball rolls under a sofa at the other end
> of the room. Girard has seen it pass under the fringe of the sofa.
> But as the sofa is deeper than the armchair . . . [he] gives up after
> a moment . . . goes right under the armchair and carefully ex-
> plores the place where the ball was before.[7]

Since Girard cannot think of the ball as an independent and permanent
body in motion, he is unable to reverse his thinking, believing that the
ball, somehow, has magically reappeared under the armchair.[8] This
thought follows what we have mentioned previously: the egocentric

thinking of the young child limits him from believing that objects and events, independent of his thinking and not in his field of view, do exist.

Around the ages of 4 or 5, children also tend to confuse age with height. This type of thinking basically says that the taller you are, the older you are. Four- and five-year-olds fail to see that aging is a continuous process in time. Therefore, the short 5-year-old believes that the tall 4-year-old is older because he is bigger. For Piaget, children at this developmental age have an egocentric and preoperational conception of succession and duration and, therefore, do not see that age differences persist throughout life:

> Filk has an older sister: "Are you the same age?" "No, because we weren't born at the same time." "Who was born first?" "She was." "Will you be the same age as her one day or will the two of you never be the same age?" "Soon I shall be bigger than her, because men are bigger than women. Then I shall be older."[9]

Compare this type of thinking to that of an 8-year-old who is able to think operationally (as opposed to preoperationally) and you will see that the order of one's birth and the ages of individuals are logically related:

> I have two small brothers, Charlie and Jean. Who was born first? Me, then Charlie and finally Jean. When you are grown up, how old will you all be? I'll be the oldest, then Charlie and then Jean. How much older will you be? The same as now. Why? It's always the same. It all depends on when one was born.[10]

For Piaget, therefore, it is not until he is 7 or 8 years of age that a child can understand "the concept of successive intervals of time corresponding to equal distances traversed successively on the face of a clock."[11] Consequently, teaching children how to tell time when they are younger than 7 or 8 years of age with the hope of any comprehension would be an exercise in futility. Except for learning by rote, children are not ready developmentally to understand how to tell time until they are in the second grade.

Chapter 8

Concluding Remarks

JUSTIFICATION

The first five years make up a small part of a child's life when compared to today's expanding life span. In terms of how the child will think, act, and feel, however, they have a significant influence. All too soon our children are teenagers and then adults. As we muse over that brief time period, we will often question how wisely we spent it with them. For it is the hope of responsible parents that each of their children will grow up to be well-adjusted citizens who will realize their potential.

Experts tell us that the years before traditional schooling are important in terms of learning intervention and parental involvement. Often the educational fate of a child is determined by what transpires during these first five years. Sometimes they are the forgotten years for some parents. Part of the problem stems from ignorance rather than indifference. What can parents do with their 2- or 5-year-old to get involved in the educational as well as the resulting emotional development that such involvement brings? Actually there are many simple and interesting things parents can do at convenient times and places. Such involvement fosters intellectual and physical growth along with the most important side effect—that someone important in their children's lives is caring about and listening to them.

Parents and educators, however, should not get involved with the type of thinking that introduces learning activities for which children are not developmentally ready. Overanxious parents and educators are not only wasting their time when they do this, but they could also be producing overanxious children who will be facing problems with feelings of insecurity throughout life:

> Working parents are more likely to be taken in by the new fads in the area of childrearing—not for bad reasons, but because they care so much and want to do all they can to make a good life for their children. They feel they must prepare their children for the pressures they feel as they work to achieve success in an overloaded life. If parents can become more relaxed about their two roles, pressures on the children may lessen.[1]

SUMMARY

Part I of this book was intended to serve as a background and introduction to Part II for parents as well as caregivers or teachers. To adequately understand the activities presented in the second half of this book, parents must first understand something about how preschool children think and learn. Particularly in the area of preschool education, it is not unusual to find parents, as well as educators, disagreeing about appropriate learning activities for preschoolers. Some of these activities might be too advanced while others are simply not appropriate.

Part I also reviewed Piaget's theory about the learning ability of preschoolers from 1 to 5 years old. The sensorimotor period, from birth to about age 2, is characterized as a time when the young child assimilates and accommodates to the world about him through his senses and body movements. A child's thinking ability during this period is limited to what the child can see or hold. A child's acquisition of language, which occurs at about 2 years of age, allows his thought processes to develop at a very rapid rate. The preoperational child is no longer limited in expression to pointing, facial gestures, or body movements. However, the thinking displayed during this period is egocentric and is characterized by the child's inability to consider the viewpoints of others.

The distinguishing trait that separates the preoperational thinker from children in the concrete operational stage is the former's inability to conserve number. In order to conserve number, a child must be developmentally ready to classify and order objects as well as count rationally. We also discussed why it is inappropriate to teach the concept of time to a preschooler and why, because of his egocentrism, the young preschooler is unable to distinguish among rigid shapes such as the circle or triangle. Therefore, a discussion of Piaget's learning theories in Part I of this book has prepared the reader for a better understanding of the rationale for the activities in Part II.

The activities in Part II are simple in content and designed to be used by parents, as well as educators and caregivers, in such convenient places as the park, in the car, or at home. They are designed to mesh with the developmental readiness of each child. Feel free to adapt and modify them as necessary, but more important, enjoy the excitement and feeling of closeness with your child that they will bring!

Part II

ACTIVITIES

Chapter 9

Before We Begin

SOME GUIDELINES

It is important that parents, educators, and caregivers provide a secure, safe, and loving environment essential to the well-being and optimal growth and development of a child. Children need many varied opportunities for emotional and social development, such as learning to share, making friends, expressing needs and wants, resolving conflicts in a constructive and assertive manner, and dealing effectively with their emotions. All these accomplishments are very important and worthwhile. The most crucial ingredient for a child in her early years of development is the opportunity to experience success, regardless of her ability and stage of development. Experiencing success is the key to instilling in children a love for learning, a thirst for knowledge, and a positive self-image.

Taking an active role in their child's learning experiences enhances the concept of parents and children learning and growing together. A child is motivated to learn by making learning fun. The power of play is believed to be extraordinary and supremely serious. It is a natural way for children to use their capacities to grow and learn many skills, as well as a positive approach to the development of a child. It is also important that, when exhibited, your child's capacity for independent effort is accepted. Young children have a strong desire to be autonomous. Therefore, they should be given this opportunity in order to prepare them for academic and social achievement in middle childhood.

FEEDBACK AND REINFORCEMENT

Children should be given feedback as often as possible. Feedback is a way of helping children to notice aspects of their behavior. It communicates to a child how she affects others. Feedback will help children keep their behavior "on target" and thus better achieve their goals. The positive strokes children are given during an activity are as beneficial as the purpose of the activity itself.

Some criteria for useful feedback:

1. It is descriptive rather than evaluative. By describing your own reaction, it leaves your child free to use it as she sees fit. Avoiding evaluative language reduces the need for your child to react defensively.
2. It is specific rather than general. To be told that you did very well will probably not be as useful as to be told that "you put that puzzle together very well" or "I like the way you are listening."
3. It takes into account the needs of both the giver and the receiver. Feedback can be destructive when it serves only our own needs and fails to consider the needs of the person on the receiving end.
4. It is directed toward behavior that the receiver can do something about. Frustration is only increased when a child is reminded of some shortcoming over which she has no control.
5. It is well timed. In general, feedback is most useful when given at the earliest opportunity after the behavior.

In addition to feedback, children also need reinforcers. Observing what their child does when she can freely choose her activities can clue parents as to what "turns her on." Utilizing what turns the child on as a reinforcer will more effectively result in positive self-esteem within the child and motivation to continue with the same type behavior. Five-minute warnings are helpful before transitions and cleanup time because they allow children time to finish what they are working on and gives them ample time to comply.

DESCRIPTION OF ACTIVITIES

Children are action-oriented learners, who need ample opportunities to play. Young children are unique individuals, with needs in all developmental areas. The wide variety of age-appropriate activities included in the following chapters are provided to stimulate learning and develop skills that draw from the curriculum areas of creative exploration, fine motor skills (manipulatives), gross motor skills, language development (expressive and receptive), mathematics, science, personal–social skills, self-help skills, and writing.

Creative exploration involves the arts. Expose your child to the activities that will enable her to create from the materials and supplies she is given. These activities allow her to express herself. Anything she designs can be considered a wonderful creation. With these activities, almost anything goes. What is important is the process, not the product.

Fine motor skills focus on eye–hand coordination that involves reaching, grasping, and manipulating objects. A sequence of fine sensorimotor behaviors using scissors, clay, puzzles, and toys are included in the various activities.

Gross motor skills examine the child's development in large muscle coordination, strength, and stamina. They involve postural reactions, balance, and ambulation. Activities utilizing play equipment as well as physical activities including hopping, running, jumping, and skipping can be found in the following chapters.

Expressive and receptive aspects of *language development* include functions such as reporting, questioning, predicting, and relating information; following and giving directions; describing actions, sources of actions, and functions; and expressing needs, feelings, and preferences. Expressive language requires verbal responses. Receptive language, on the other hand, does not require verbal responses.

Mathematics and science address intellectual functions such as reasoning, problem solving, and knowledge. The specific skills included in these activities, such as numbers, colors, shapes, money, and measurements, are basic prerequisites to scholastic functioning.

Personal–social skills reflect the child's perception and knowledge of her personal life and examines interpersonal behaviors such as the ability to relate to others, sensitivity to others, helpfulness, and cooperation. The personal–social activities focus on the child's responsiveness to her social environment.

Self-help skills involve the child's ability to independently and responsibly deal with the skills of daily living. The activities in this section assist with learning skills, such as feeding, dressing, toileting, bathing, and grooming.

Writing skills are a primary focus of the child's early school years because the written language constitutes a basic form of communication in society. The writing activities in this book are aimed at addressing the stages of grasping writing instruments, the role of finger and easel painting, and a hierarchy of *prewriting skills* for appropriate developmental levels. Proper development of fine motor skills is essential to ensure a successful initial writing experience.

Instilling a motivation to learn during early childhood can benefit children during their later years of education. From 1 to 5 years of age are the critical years in a person's life. Make these years positive ones for your child. Spend "quality" time with your child and watch her grow and learn. There is so much around us to be observed and acted upon. Be a guiding light for your child. *Learn with your preschooler.*

A CHILD'S PLEA TO HIS PARENTS

Give me more than food to nourish me. Give me the warmth and the security of your love.

Let me enjoy all five senses. Give me plenty of things to look at, to feel, to smell, to listen to, to taste. And even some things to break.

Teach me to take my turn. Watch me play so you can see how I am trying to work out my problems and what I am up against.

When you tell me to do something, please tell me why I should do it. Let me feel that I am a contributing member of the family. And be sure to include me in making the family plans when you can.

Please don't keep me your baby when I want to feel grown up. Don't transfer your fears to me. I have enough of my own to cope with and I don't need any more.

Help me not to act when I am angry. But don't make me so afraid of showing anger that I lose my capacity to feel strongly about anything.

Let me learn bit by bit to bear pain, to want things but to be strong enough to postpone gratification of certain feelings I am not ready to experience.

Let me try out my new powers as my body develops—to creep, to stand, to walk, climb, jump, and run when I am ready. Don't limit the natural needs of my body because you have some unresolved hang-ups.

Give me a little corner in the house that is all mine and nobody else's. I need moments of peace and quiet that cannot be invaded by anyone.

Give me my share of consideration and attention. I must know every day, even if for just a few moments, that I am the only one you are thinking about and loving.

Let me ask any question that pops into my head.

Don't make me ashamed for having asked it, even if it seems stupid. And give me as honest an answer as you can. If you don't know the answer, please say so. It's good training to hear someone say "I don't know, but I will try to find out for you."

Be patient with me when I don't do things very well at first. Remember, I have so many things to learn and almost everything takes some practice.

Above all, grant me, without reservation, your debt to me—unconditional love. For if I know it is there, I will be able to give the same to my children—and they will be able to give it to their children.

YOUR CHILD
(Author Unknown)

Chapter 10

Activities at Home

LEARNING CENTER IDEAS

Dr. Seuss created *The Cat in the Hat* for a rainy day of entertainment in the home of "Sally and I." But I wouldn't dare suggest that you bring "Thing One" and "Thing Two" into your home. Try setting up learning centers or areas of interest throughout your home. It is a creative way to transform your home into a productive world for your child. These areas will provide an opportunity for your child to choose constructive activities that are appropriate for her level of skill and interest:

1. Participation in activities with *puzzles and manipulative toys* includes practice of fine motor skills (small muscles), eye–hand coordination, recognition of shape and color, practice solving problems, and opportunity for creativity. Help your child find enough space in which to engage in these activities, either on the floor or at a table. Your child may need help in selecting a puzzle or toy. Encourage your child when she needs help. Put in a few crucial pieces of a puzzle if necessary for your child, but don't do it all unless placing pieces herself is frustrating for your child. Encourage your child to clean up one activity before choosing another.

2. Set up a comfortable and quiet area for *reading books and listening to tapes and records*. Supervise your child when he is using a record player or tape recorder. Allow your child to wear headphones if you have them. There are books available in stores that sell tapes that go with

certain books. Encourage your child to listen to the tape while looking at the book.

When you are reading a book to your child, it is helpful if you are familiar with the story before reading it. Make introductory remarks to get your child's interest. Comment on the cover, pictures, titles, colors on the cover, and so forth. Each time you read a book, discuss whether that book is a hardback or paperback. Show her the title page and call it that. Have your child say "title page." Your child will have books that she prefers. She will want them read over and over again. Show interest and enthusiasm even after the third reading in a row.

3. The *housekeeping center* provides an opportunity for children to act out real-life experiences, try out adult roles, and practice important language skills. Children enjoy having adults participate in playing restaurant, and so on. You may initiate this type of play when there is a need. Washing and drying dishes, playing with dolls, and "cooking" with play dough will be fun for the children. Encourage your child to help in cleaning up this area when playtime is over. Utilize it as someplace special for your child to pretend he is going. Change it periodically for variety and to provide opportunities for experience through dramatic play. Here are some ideas:

- *Shopping at the supermarket.* Provide empty cans and boxes of food, play money, purse/wallet, play cash register.
- *Doctor, doctor.* Provide dolls, tongue depressors, Popsicle sticks (makes a great thermometer), cotton balls, old white shirt. To make a stethoscope, put a piece of string through a piece of egg carton (Fig. 10-1).
- *Bakery.* Provide cookie cutters, cookie sheets, play dough, spoons, measuring cups, cash register, eggbeaters, lunch bags, play money.

4. *Block building* will help your child translate her experiences into play. Blocks are tools that stimulate the imagination and develop coordination. Help your child start building. Give her encouragement and suggestions, but do not dominate block play. Interesting placement of a few blocks may initiate play. Small cars, animals, and trains are fun to incorporate into block building.

Figure 10-1

5. *Art* reveals your child's creativity. Show an interest in your child's work. When your child completes a project, do not ask what he made. He may not know and should not be made to think that it should be "something." Display your child's work around the house.

ACTIVITIES

The activities in this chapter cover the various subject areas described in the introductory chapter of Part II. At the beginning of this section, you will find recipes for making various items such as play dough, clay, and magic goop. These are great for enabling your child to develop fine motor skills. Allow your child to assist in making the recipes so that she can learn about measuring and mixing items together. Demonstrate play activities or suggest new ways for her to enjoy toys and play materials when necessary. Be sure that the toys are safe and appropriate for the child's stage of development.

Recipes

Refrigerate each of the following when it is not in use:

1. *Clay*

   1 1/2 cups warm water
   1 cup salt
   4 cups flour
   Optional: food coloring (add to water before mixing in other ingredients)

2. *Magic Goop*

   2 cups cornstarch
   1 cup water
   Optional: food coloring (add to water before mixing in other ingredients)

3. *Peanut Butter Play Clay*

   2 cups creamy peanut butter
   2 cups powdered milk
   1 cup honey

4. *Play Dough*

   2 cups flour
   1 cup salt
   1 cup water
   oil
   Optional: Food coloring (add to water before mixing in other ingredients)

Creative Exploration (2–5 Years Old)

A Scrap of Art

SUBJECT:	Creative exploration
LEVEL:	2 years old and up
PURPOSE:	Create with scraps
	Develop small muscle ability

MATERIALS: Scraps of any sort, i.e., paper, material, feathers, yarn
Glue
Paper

PROCEDURE: Give the child a piece of paper. Place various pieces of scraps in front of the child. Tell the child to glue on pieces to make any design he would like. Display his art when he completes it.

A Sandy Design

SUBJECT: Creative exploration

LEVEL: 3 years old and up

PURPOSE: Create picture with sand–paint mixture

MATERIALS: Sand
Dry powder paint
Container with a shaker lid (i.e., old spice container)
Glue
Heavy paper (i.e., cardboard)

PROCEDURE: Mix sand with powdered paint. Put in container with shaker lid. Have the child make a design on her paper with the glue. Shake sand–paint mixture on the glue design. Shake off excess sand–paint. Let dry. Display the child's creation.

Marbleized Painting

SUBJECT: Creative exploration

LEVEL: 3 years old and up

PURPOSE: Create design with marble and paint
Eye–hand coordination
Hand manipulation
Develop small muscle ability

MATERIALS: Shoe box lid
Paper to fit inside of lid

Marble
Tempera paint
Spoon

PROCEDURE: Have the child fit the paper into the shoe box lid. Give
him a spoon. Have him put the marble on the spoon,
then have him put the marble in paint and take it out
with the spoon. Put marble in shoe box lid and have the
child move the lid around to make a design (Fig. 10-2).

VARIATIONS: Replace marble with golf ball or super ball

Paint with Straws

SUBJECT: Creative exploration

LEVEL: 3 years old and up

Figure 10-2

PURPOSE: Creative painting with straws
                 Breath control

MATERIALS: Tempera paint
                 Straws
                 Paper

PROCEDURE:

- Practice blowing through straw first. Demonstrate to the child. Have the child do it. Hold your hand in front of her straw to feel if she is blowing out air.
- Put paper in front of the child. Have a piece of paper for yourself to use for demonstration
- Make sure paint is "liquidy." Put a small amount on the sheet of paper in one spot. Put your straw to your mouth and aim it toward the paint. Be sure not to touch the paint with your straw. Blow through your straw to cause paint to move and create a design.
- Put some paint on the child's paper. Tell her to put the straw to her mouth and point it toward the paint. Allow her to get close to, but not touch, the paint. Tell the child to blow into the straw to move the paint around on the paper. If the child has trouble blowing, demonstrate blowing in an exaggerated fashion. Add different colors if you wish.
- Allow the painting to dry, then display it in the house.

Sponge Painting

SUBJECT: Creative exploration

LEVEL: 3 years old and up

PURPOSE: Create by painting with sponges
                 Develop small muscle ability

MATERIALS: Sponges of different shapes
                 Paper
                 Tempera paint

Clothespins

Container of water

PROCEDURE: Use clothespins as a holder for the sponges. Assist the child as needed. Attach clothespin to the sponge (Fig. 10-3). Dip the sponge into the water. Dip the sponge into the paint. Stamp sponge on paper however you like.

NOTE: Younger children will need assistance with routine of getting the design on the paper: attach sponge, sponge in water, sponge in paint, stamp on paper.

Feather Painting

SUBJECT: Creative exploration

LEVEL: 4 and 5 years old

Figure 10-3

PURPOSE:	Creative design by painting with feathers Develop small muscle ability Prewriting skills
MATERIALS:	Feathers (if you can't find any individual feathers, buy a cheap feather duster and pull apart) Tempera paint
PROCEDURE:	Dip feather into paint and make a design on paper. Let dry and hang up to display.
VARIATION:	Have the children paint to music.

Fine Motor Skills (1–5 Years old)

Cube in a Cup

SUBJECT:	Fine motor skills
LEVEL:	1 year old
PURPOSE:	Develop ability to place small objects into larger objects
MATERIALS:	8 1-inch cubes Shallow box Cup
PROCEDURE:	Demonstrate how to put a cube in the box, then have the child put a cube in the box. Tell him to continue until all the cubes are in the box. Remove the cubes from the box. Put the box to the side. Place a cup in front of the child. Demonstrate how to put a cube in the cup. Tell the child to put a cube in the cup. Continue until all the cubes are in the cup.
VARIATIONS:	Toys in the toy box Stacking cups—one inside the other, from largest to smallest . Grocery items in the grocery cart Baby doll in the baby doll carriage

Playing the Spoons

SUBJECT:	Fine motor skills
LEVEL:	1 year old
PURPOSE:	Develop ability to beat two spoons together
MATERIALS:	Two spoons (not plastic)
PROCEDURE:	• Place one spoon in each hand of the child. Make sure she has a grip on the spoons.
	• Demonstrate beating two spoons together to the child. Tell her to watch you.
	• Assist the child in beating the two spoons together (Fig. 10-4).
	• Let go of the child's hands and encourage her to keep doing it. Immediately reinforce the child by clapping and/or cheering when she successfully beats the spoons together.

Figure 10-4

VARIATION: Put on a record or the radio and play the spoons with the music.

Tower Straight Up

SUBJECT: Fine motor skills

LEVEL: 1 1/2 years old

PURPOSE: Develop ability to stack three to four blocks, one on top of the other, without falling

MATERIALS: 4 blocks

PROCEDURE: Demonstrate placing one block on top of the other. Then, place one block on the floor and hand the child a block. Tell the child to put the block on top of the block on the floor. Point to where you want her to put the block. Be sure to praise her for each time she puts a block on the stack. Continue to hand her one block at a time until she initiates picking the blocks up by herself. Knocking down the tower can be just as much fun.

Turning Pages One by One

SUBJECT: Fine motor skills

LEVEL: 1 1/2 to 2 years old

PURPOSE: Develop ability to turn pages of a book one at a time

MATERIALS: Books with pages of average thickness

PROCEDURE: Demonstrate turning pages one by one with a book. Turn the pages and talk about the pictures. Make a "beep" sound each time you are ready to turn the page. Continue to talk about the pictures or reading the book to the child. Tell the child "Turn the page, beep." Give the child praise when he turns one page.

NOTE: See the activity, "My Book of Photos" (p. 77). Make one for your child and he may never want to put it

down. Great book of interest for him to develop fine
motor abilities in turning pages.

Build the Tower and Down It Goes

SUBJECT:	Fine motor skills
LEVEL:	1 1/2 years old and up
PURPOSE:	Develop small muscle ability
	Coordination
MATERIALS:	Building blocks or stackable cups
PROCEDURE:	Have the child build a tower with the blocks. Assist the child as needed. Encourage the child to keep building the tower until it falls or the child may choose to knock it down herself. Start building again until it falls or is knocked down. Praise the child as she builds the blocks and knocks them down.
	Goals for building a tower: 1 1/2 years old—three to four blocks; 3 years old—ten blocks.
NOTE:	See the activity, "Road Design" below as an interesting follow-up.

Road Design

SUBJECT:	Fine motor skills
LEVEL:	1 1/2 years old and up
PURPOSE:	Develop small muscle ability
	Opportunity for dramatic play and imagination
MATERIALS:	Old solid-colored tablecloth or sheet
	Permanent markers
	Blocks
	Small cars, trucks, tractors, airplanes, etc.
	Small wooden figures of people, street signs, etc.

PROCEDURE: Draw a road design on the tablecloth with the permanent markers. Add trees, flowers, and any other things you would like to add. Allow to dry (Fig. 10-5). Encourage the child to use this for dramatic play with blocks, cars, trucks, people, street signs, etc. He can create his own little town making buildings with the blocks (Fig. 10-6).

Manipulating Clay

SUBJECT: Fine motor skills

LEVEL: 2 years old

PURPOSE: Develop small muscle ability
Hand manipulation

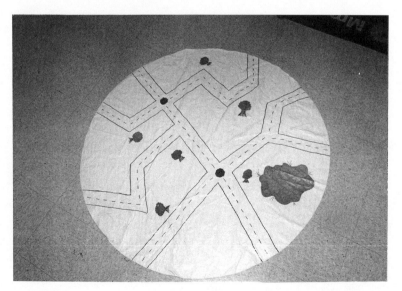

Figure 10-5

Figure 10-6

MATERIALS: Clay (for recipe, see p. 60)
             Placemats (for easy cleanup)

PROCEDURE: Encourage the child to play with the clay. Make balls, snakes, pancakes, etc., as the child watches. Tell the child to make a ball. Assist the child as needed. Then let the child squeeze the ball. Tell the child to make a snake. Show her how to roll it as needed. Tell the child to make a pancake. Pound the clay to make it as flat as possible. Assist the child as needed.

NOTE: If clay is too hard, the child may use play dough, which has a softer consistency.

Puffy Clouds

SUBJECT: Fine motor skills

LEVEL: 2 1/2 years old and up

PURPOSE: Develop small muscle ability
Learn about clouds
Creativity

MATERIALS: Cotton balls
Paper
Glue
Crayons, colored pencils, markers, or paint

PROCEDURE: Talk to the child about the clouds in the sky. Show them to the child on a cloudy day. Tell him you would like him to make a picture with puffy clouds in it. Give the child some cotton balls and tell him that he is to make the clouds. Give him the glue to put the cotton on the paper. Assist the child as needed. Encourage the child to draw things on the paper that are outside, i.e., the sun, flowers, birds, trees, grass.

NOTE: This can be used as a follow-up for the activity in Chapter 11, "Story in the Sky" (pp. 173–174).

Form Board Fun

SUBJECT: Fine motor skills

LEVEL: 3 years old

PURPOSE: Develop ability to put three shapes (circle, square, triangle) in a form board

MATERIALS: Form board
Triangle, circle, and square (Fig. 10-7). *To make shapes:* Use heavy cardboard. Cut the shapes and color each a different color. *To make form board:* Use heavy cardboard. Cut the holes slightly larger than the shape. Color each hole with the color of the matching shape to make it easier for the child to see.

PROCEDURE: Demonstrate placing shapes in appropriate hole. Give shape to the child to do it. Assist as needed. Name the shapes that are being used.

Figure 10-7

Caterpillar

SUBJECT:	Fine motor skills
LEVEL:	3 years old and up
PURPOSE:	Develop small muscle ability
MATERIALS:	Egg carton Scissors Paint Cotton balls 2 pipe cleaners
PROCEDURE:	Cut off lid of egg carton. Cut carton in half lengthwise (Fig. 10-8). Dab carton with paint using cotton balls. Insert pipe cleaners at front end of egg carton for antennas (Fig. 10-9).

Lion Face

SUBJECT:	Fine motor skills
LEVEL:	3, 4, and 5 years old
PURPOSE:	Develop ability to cut with scissors
MATERIALS:	Paper plate Scissors Construction paper: blue, black, brown, red Crayons: brown, yellow Glue

Figure 10-8

PROCEDURE: As the child watches, begin to cut around the outside of the paper plate to fray the edges. Allow the child to cut until the paper plate has been cut all the way around. Cut out blue eyes, a brown nose, and a red mouth for the lion. Have the child do it with your assistance as needed. Allow the child to glue the eyes, nose, and mouth onto the plate. Have the child cut six black whiskers with your assistance as needed. Have the child color the paper plate with brown and yellow crayons. Have the child glue the whiskers on the lion (Fig. 10-10).

Figure 10-9

Figure 10-10

Make a Germ

SUBJECT:	Fine motor skills
LEVEL:	3, 4, and 5 years old
PURPOSE:	Develop fine motor ability
	Develop some understanding of what a germ is like
MATERIALS:	Clay (see recipe, p. 60)
	Tempera paint and a paint brush
	Oven
PROCEDURE:	• Talk to the child about the importance of cleanliness. Talk to her about why we shouldn't put objects or our fingers in our mouth. Tell the child that we collect germs when we put these things in our mouth. Continue by telling the child that you can't see a germ but they are all around us. That is also why we should cover our mouth when we sneeze or cough, then wash our hands.
	• Now say something like this: "Let's pretend we can see a germ. I don't think it would look very pretty. Let's get some clay and make it into a funny shape, something like we might think a germ looks like. Then we can cook it in the oven. When it cools off, we'll paint it."

- Proceed by making the clay into funny shapes. Bake it at 275 degrees for 3 hours. Allow it to cool, then paint it with the tempera paints. When completed, tell the child that this will be her reminder of germs since we really can't see them.

VARIATION: Shape clay into different symbols for holidays and paint them after baking. They will make creative decorations or gifts for the holidays.

Make a Necklace

SUBJECT:	Fine motor skills
LEVEL:	3, 4, and 5 years old
PURPOSE:	Develop ability to string items Develop small muscle ability
MATERIALS:	Shoestrings Straws, fruit loops, paper towel rolls, macaroni Scissors
PROCEDURE:	Tie a large knot at one end of shoestring. Cut paper towel rolls to make round "beads." Put hole through sides of round beads (Fig. 10-11). Cut straws into 1/2- to 1-inch pieces. Place items between you and the child. As the child watches, hold the string in your hand and push a "bead" over the end of the string. Slide it down to the knotted end. Allow the child to do the next one. Assist the child as needed until the child can do it independently.

Make Your Own Book

SUBJECT:	Fine motor skills
LEVEL:	3, 4, and 5 years old
PURPOSE:	Develop ability to fold and crease paper Develop ability to grasp and manipulate objects Develop ability to cut with scissors

Figure 10-11

MATERIALS: Construction paper or paper with some thickness to it
              Glue
              Old magazines
              Scissors

PROCEDURE: • Pick a topic of things that most children like. For ex-
                ample, let's go with animals. Have the child look
                through the magazines for animals. Cut out the ani-
                mals as you find them. Assist the child with cutting
                as needed.
              • Fold construction paper in half, using about four
                pages. Put together to make a book. Title the book
                on the front page. Allow the child to glue pictures
                throughout the book wherever she would like.
              • Ask the child if she would like to say anything about

the pictures in the book. Write down the "story" the child tells you. Read the book together several times.

VARIATIONS: 1. *Number Book:* Help the child write the number. Have the child glue the number of pictures on the page to match the numeral (i.e., 1 person, 2 shoes, 3 cars, etc.). Encourages the development of counting objects.

2. *Alphabet Book:* Help the child write each letter of the alphabet. Make sure you have folded enough pieces of construction paper for the entire alphabet. Have the child find pictures that begin with that letter. Cut out the pictures from the old magazines as you find them. Assist the child as necessary. Work on it a little at a time. Have the child glue the pictures that go with the correct letter.

My Book of Photos

SUBJECT: Fine motor skills

LEVEL: 3, 4, and 5 years old

PURPOSE: Develop small muscle ability

MATERIALS: 10 pieces of cardboard approximately 5 x 7 inches or larger
Hole puncher
Yarn
Glue
Photos of family and friends

PROCEDURE: • Have the child pick out pictures of family and friends that he would like in his own book of photos. Glue the pictures to the cardboard pieces. Make it into a book by punching two to three holes along the left side of the cardboard pages. Pull yarn through and tie.

• Have the child design a cover for the book before putting it all together.

- Encourage the child to turn the pages one at a time to develop his small muscle ability.

Q-Tip Painting

SUBJECT: Fine motor skills

LEVEL: 3 years old and up

PURPOSE: Develop small muscle ability
Coordination
Creativity

MATERIALS: Tempera paints (mix well with a small amount of flaked detergent such as Ivory Snow; this will help easy cleanup)
Q-tips
Paper
Smock (optional—helps protect clothing)

PROCEDURE: • Set out tempera paint(s) for the child. Give the child a piece of paper. Set a Q-tip with each color paint if you are using a variety. For the younger child, it would be best to start with one color at a time.
- Demonstrate to the child on your own paper by dipping a Q-tip into paint. Make a design on your paper. Tell the child to make a picture on her paper. Assist as needed. Praise her as she works.
- When she is finished with her creation, allow it to dry. Display for everyone to enjoy.

Three-Dimensional Clown

SUBJECT: Fine motor skills

LEVEL: 3, 4, and 5 years old

PURPOSE: Develop small muscle ability

MATERIALS: Tissue paper—various colors, small pieces
Construction paper or posterboard
Glue (small bottle for child to handle)
Thin marker

Figure 10-12

PROCEDURE: Draw a picture of a clown on construction paper. Make it large enough for the child to cover it with small crumbled pieces of tissue paper. Have the child crumble the tissue paper and glue the pieces onto the outfit of the clown (Fig. 10-12). Demonstrate first for the child. Assist the child as needed.

VARIATION: *Tracking activity:* Print a word for the child (i.e., his name or any word he chooses). Have the child go over the letters with glue, following them as they would be written. Assist the child as needed. Have the child crumble the tissue paper into small balls. Assist the child in gluing the tissue paper onto the word from left to right as the word would be written with a writing tool (Fig. 10-13).

Figure 10-13

Gross Motor Skills (1 1/2–5 Years Old)

Picking It Up without Falling Down

SUBJECT: Gross motor skills

LEVEL: 1 1/2 years old

PURPOSE: Practice balance
Develop listening skills and following directions

MATERIALS: Pillows from family room

PROCEDURE: Place pillow on floor. While the child is watching, stoop to the floor to pick up the pillow without falling down. Have the child pick up the pillow as you did and put it on the sofa or chair. Allow the child to do it several times.

Push Me–Pull Me

SUBJECT: Gross motor skills

LEVEL: 1 1/2 years old

PURPOSE: Develop ability to push or pull large, lightweight objects
Teach the child words and actions

MATERIALS: Pull toys—with strings or yarn
Large empty box
Empty laundry basket

PROCEDURE: • Demonstrate to the child by pulling a toy. Tell the child to "pull" the toy.
• Demonstrate to the child by pushing the box. Tell the child to "push" the box. Do the same with the empty laundry basket. Allow the child to put some of her favorite toys in the basket and push it around.

Up and Down the Stairs

SUBJECT: Gross motor skills

LEVEL: 1 1/2 years old and up

PURPOSE: Develop child's ability to move up and down stairs
Practice balance and coordination

MATERIALS: Small staircase

PROCEDURE: *Down:* 1. Start with "boom-boom." Have the child sit
on his bottom at the top of the staircase. Sit down next
to him. Demonstrate "boom-boom" by shifting your
bottom down one step (Fig. 10-14). Now tell him to do
it and say "boom-boom." Practice all the way down the

Figure 10-14

staircase. Encourage the child to do it slowly. Show him how to use his feet for support.

2. Next, teach the child to creep backward down the steps (Fig. 10-15). Demonstrate to the child how to go down using hands and knees. Have the child do it. Help him with knee and hand positions. Start on a small staircase or at the bottom two steps. Slowly increase the number of steps.

Figure 10-15

3. Last, teach the child how to walk down the steps one step at a time (both feet on one step before going to the next) holding on to the railing and/or your hand (Fig. 10-16). Do not begin this step until the child is walking with good balance and coordination.

Up: 1. Demonstrate crawling up the steps with your hands and knees. Tell the child to do it. Help him with knee and hand positions as needed (Fig. 10-17).

Figure 10-16

Figure 10-17

2. Next, teach the child to walk up the steps one at a time (with both feet on one step before going on to the next step) holding onto the railing and/or your hand (Fig. 10-18).

VARIATION: *Down:* Teach the concept of down and counting numbers by saying "Down 1, 2, 3, etc."
Up: Teach the concept of up and counting numbers by saying "Up 1, 2, 3, etc."

CAUTION: • Slowly increase number of steps.
      • Stay with the child at all times when he is going up
        or down steps.
      • Be sure steps are clear of any objects before using
        them. A good rule of thumb is to always keep the
        steps clear of objects.

Figure 10-18

Sweep the Floor

SUBJECT: Gross motor skills

LEVEL: 2 years old and up

PURPOSE: Develop large muscle ability
Coordination
Cooperation

MATERIALS: Child-sized broom and dust pan

PROCEDURE: When it's time to sweep, allow the child to help you. Give her the small broom. Demonstrate with your broom. The child will just follow along. It will take her some practice to get it right. Give her time and encourage her to do her best as she goes along. She may end up making more of a mess rather than actually helping, but praise her for a job well done. It will encourage her to keep practicing.

In and Out of the Box

SUBJECT: Gross motor skills

LEVEL: 2 1/2 years old and up

PURPOSE: Develop the ability to climb in and out of a box
Learn meaning of prepositions "in" and "out"

MATERIALS: Box about 10 inches high

PROCEDURE: Demonstrate to the child as you climb into the box "See, I am climbing IN the box." Climb out of the box as you say to the child, "I am climbing OUT of the box." Now tell the child, "Climb IN the box." Assist the child as needed. Then tell the child, "Climb OUT of the box." Assist the child as needed.

May I Bring You Your Order?

SUBJECT: Gross motor skills/Dramatic play

LEVEL: 3 years old

PURPOSE: Develop ability to carry a tray without dropping the objects on it
Coordination
Balance

MATERIALS: Tray
Unbreakable objects (i.e., play dough, plastic cups, paper plates)

PROCEDURE: Play restaurant with the child. Have the child serve you as a waiter by carrying a tray of unbreakable items to you. Then have him place the tray on the table and give you the items. Assist the child as needed.

Up on the Tightwire

SUBJECT: Gross motor skills

LEVEL: 3 years old (5 years old—see "Variation")

PURPOSE: Develop balance

MATERIALS: Masking tape, 10 feet long

PROCEDURE: Place masking tape on floor or carpet. Demonstrate walking on the masking tape with one foot in front of the other. Place arms out at sides to help keep balance. Have the child do it. Allow the child to hold a long stick and let her pretend to be in a circus on the tightwire.

VARIATION: 5 years old: Have the child walk backward in a straight line for four steps (or more), placing her toe approximately 1 inch (or less) behind her heel.

Beanbag Toss

SUBJECT: Gross motor skills

LEVEL: 3 years old and up

PURPOSE: Develop ability to throw overhead

MATERIALS: Beanbag or beanball (to make a beanbag, put dry beans in a nylon stocking and tie it securely)
Laundry basket

PROCEDURE: Demonstrate throwing a beanbag or beanball overhand into the laundry basket. Now tell the child it is his turn. Start with basket close to the child and gradually move basket farther away.

Up the Stairs with Alternating Feet

SUBJECT: Gross motor skills

LEVEL: 3 years old and up

PURPOSE: Develop ability to go up steps, alternating feet

MATERIALS: *Footprints:* left foot—make with red paper; right foot—make with green paper
Red and green stickers
Stairway

PROCEDURE: • Place red and green feet on the floor. Be sure that red foot is on the left and green foot on the right. Place a red sticker on the child's left foot and a green sticker on her right foot. Have the child walk the footprints, matching color of footprint to color sticker on her foot. Practice on the floor until the child has successfully completed this process.
• Move footprints onto stairway. Start with only two steps at a time and slowly increase.
   Goals: 3 years old—two steps; 4 years old—three steps up and down; 5 years old—steps of a playground ladder (unassisted).

Don't Spill a Drop

SUBJECT: Gross motor skills

LEVEL: 4 years old

PURPOSE: Develop ability to carry liquid in a cup (filled 1 inch from the top) without spilling
Coordination
Balance

MATERIALS: Cup
                   Beverage, i.e., water, juice, milk

PROCEDURE: Start with water if you prefer so nothing will get ruined. The cup should not be very full at the beginning. Pour a beverage in a cup for the child. Have the child carry it to a table close by. Gradually lengthen the distance of where he is to carry the cup of liquid. Gradually increase amount of liquid in cup up to 1 inch from the top.

Language Development (1–5 Years old)

Jabber, Jabber

SUBJECT: Language development

LEVEL: 1 year old

PURPOSE: Expose language patterns to the child

MATERIALS: None

PROCEDURE:
- Talk to the child during normal activities of the day (changing diaper, dressing, feeding, bathing, playing). It's okay if the child doesn't understand you. This helps the child learn language patterns and the importance of language.
- Sing to the child. Read simple picture books to the child on a daily basis. A routine story time is very beneficial for the child. It is a great winding down activity before bedtime.

Pillow Talk

SUBJECT: Language development

LEVEL: 1 year old and up

PURPOSE: Promote language development
                   Bonding

MATERIALS: Large pillow

PROCEDURE: When ready for quiet time, throw a large pillow on the floor. Have the child lay down with you on the pillow. Give your undivided attention to the child. Talk with her, cuddle, read a story. Enjoy the moments with the child. Great "quality" time with the child.

Telephone Conversation

SUBJECT: Language development

LEVEL: 2 1/2 years old

PURPOSE: Develop skills to talk on telephone
Listening and responding

MATERIALS: Two toy telephones and a bell

PROCEDURE: Give one telephone to the child and you hold onto the other. Tell the child that when you ring the bell, he needs to pick up his telephone and say hello. Ring the bell. When the child answers the phone, say hello. Carry on a conversation with the child as you normally would during any telephone conversation. Ask the child questions. Give him ample time to answer. Have the child talk to Grandma and Grandpa on the phone. Prompt him if necessary. Give suggestions of things for him to say. Before you know it, he will be holding a conversation on his own.

Alphabet Book

SUBJECT: Language development

LEVEL: 3, 4, and 5 years old

PURPOSE: Develop letter recognition
Encourage language development

MATERIALS: Construction paper
Old magazines

Scissors
Glue

PROCEDURE: See the activity, "Make Your Own Book: Variations" (p. 77).

Bakery

SUBJECT: Language development

LEVEL: 3 1/2 years old and up

PURPOSE: Develop language skills through dramatic play
Learn about different things at a bakery

MATERIALS: Cookie cutters
Cookie sheets
Play dough
Spoons, measuring cups
Cash register
Eggbeaters
Lunch bags
Play money

PROCEDURE: Help the child set up the bakery. Teach the child what each item is and what it is used for. Demonstrate the use of the materials to the child. Have the child be the customer and you be the baker. Act out the parts. After a short time, switch roles.

Post Office

SUBJECT: Language development

LEVEL: 3 1/2 years and up

PURPOSE: Develop language skills through dramatic play
Learn about things in a post office

MATERIALS: Index cards
Ink pads
Rubber stamps

Used envelopes
Stamps
Crayons, pencils
Boxes with slits

PROCEDURE: Help the child set up the post office with all the materials. Demonstrate to the child what each thing is used for. Let the child try it. Allow the child to be the postmaster in the post office and you be a customer. Act out your part and encourage the child as you go. Switch parts after awhile.

This Is What Happened

SUBJECT: Language development

LEVEL: 4 years old

PURPOSE: Develop ability to give account of recent experiences in order of occurrence

MATERIALS: None

PROCEDURE: At the end of an experience or the end of the day, talk with the child about what she did. Ask the child "What did you do today that you liked the most?" "Where did you go after breakfast today?"

VARIATIONS: Use three or four pictures for the child to put in order of occurrence. Assist the child as needed. As the child successfully completes this, you can increase the number of pictures.

Call for Help

SUBJECT: Language development

LEVEL: 4 years old and up

PURPOSE: Teach the child how to contact someone in case of an emergency

MATERIALS: Toy phone

PROCEDURE: • Teach the child her full name
            • Teach the child to dial 911. Explain to her that this
              is the number to call if she ever needs anyone to help
              her. Have her say the following on the phone after
              dialing: "My name is Melissa Hauck and I need
              help." Reward the child for doing a good job. Prac-
              tice this several times.
            • Encourage the child to look at what is around her so
              she may describe it on the phone if she doesn't know
              the name of where she is. It is important to talk to
              the child when you go places, telling her where you
              are. Teach the child her street address. Go over and
              over it. Teach your child her home phone number.
              If the child is able to read numbers and transfer each
              number to the phone, have it written down for her
              to carry with her.
            • Teach the child your full name. Make sure she
              knows names of family members.

I Know My Senses

SUBJECT: Language development
LEVEL: 5 years old
PURPOSE: Develop ability to identify use of senses
MATERIALS: None
PROCEDURE: Teach the child the following (point to each part of
            your body as you say it):

> I see with my eyes—LOOK
>   Look, see the clouds in the sky.
> I hear with my ears—LISTEN
>   Listen, hear the birds singing.
> I smell with my nose—BREATHE
>   Breathe in, smell the pretty flowers.
> I taste with my mouth—EAT
>   Eat, taste the delicious pizza.

I touch with my hands—FEEL
Feel, touch the cute puppy, so soft.

VARIATION: Make matching cards with each of the following on it:

Eyes	Clouds in the sky
Ears	Birds
Nose	Flower
Mouth	Pizza
Hands	Puppy

Ask the child:

What do you look with? What do you see?
What do you listen with? What do you hear?
What do you breathe with? What do you smell?
What do you taste with? What do you eat?
What do you feel with? What do you touch?

Picture Story

SUBJECT: Language development

LEVEL: 5 years old

PURPOSE: Develop ability to tell a story by looking at and describing pictures

MATERIALS: Story books with pictures

PROCEDURE: Children need to have many books available to them. Always keep the old and familiar, and gradually introduce new books to them. Make reading stories a regular part of every day. Children will become familiar with books that you read to them several times. The pictures are a guide. Read a book to the child at least once a day. If the story is too long for the child's attention span, make up your own words. Talk about the pictures together, naming actions and objects. After reading the same book several times with the child, have him tell the story as you turn the page to new pictures.

NOTE: For a follow-up activity, see "Picture Story" (p. 198).

Mathematics (1–5 Years Old)

Counting Fingers and Toes

SUBJECT:	Mathematics
LEVEL:	1 year old and up
PURPOSE:	Develop ability to count to ten
	Learn body parts: fingers and toes
MATERIALS:	Washcloth
	Bathtub
PROCEDURE:	This is a fun activity for meal cleanup and bath time. Begin by singing the following verse:

> Wiggle, wiggle fingers.
> Wiggle, wiggle toes.
> Oh let's count them,
> Ready, set, go . . .

While washing the child's fingers, wash one finger at a time while counting them. Do the same with the child's toes.

Feel for It

SUBJECT:	Mathematics/Classification
LEVEL:	3 years old
PURPOSE:	Reinforce the meanings of words of comparison and position
MATERIALS:	"Feel Box"
	Items from around the house such as a straw and a pencil, a ball and an inflated balloon, fake fur and sandpaper, two blocks of different sizes, a fork and a

spoon, a hat and a mitten, a doll's shoe and the child's shoe.

PROCEDURE: Place two items inside the box. Ask, "Can you find the one that is" longer (or harder, or hollow); heavier (or larger, or softer); rough (or feels best); smaller; used to eat ice cream; worn on your head; too small for you.

Which Doesn't Belong?

SUBJECT: Mathematics/Classification

LEVEL: 3 years old

PURPOSE: Help children notice differences

MATERIALS: Sets of three objects, one of which is different from the other two such as two picture books, one coloring book; two different shoes and a sneaker; dollhouse furniture—chair, sofa, and a table; a rake, a hoe, and a hammer.

PROCEDURE: Ask the child to pick out the one that doesn't belong with the other two.

Birthday Cakes

SUBJECT: Mathematics/Counting

LEVEL: 3 years old

PURPOSE: Develop the concept of ordinal numbers

MATERIALS: Picture cards of birthday cakes with one, two, three, and four candles
Picture cards of children whose ages correspond (dolls may be used)

PROCEDURE: After discussing the cakes and counting the candles, have the child arrange the cards in order. Stress that "On your first birthday you are 1 year old" and ask the child to choose the doll (or picture) that corresponds.

Proceed with emphasis on the relationship of second and the number 2.

NOTE: While every child seems to know the meaning of "first," the words "first" and "second" give no oral clue to their relationship to "one" and "two." The above activity stresses this correspondence.

Fill 'em Up

SUBJECT: Mathematics/Counting

LEVEL: 3 years old

PURPOSE: Develop the concept of a one-to-one correspondence

MATERIALS: A large carton (24-egg capacity) with a line drawn down the center
Ten or twelve envelopes containing anywhere from zero to four cardboard disks

PROCEDURE: Have the child in turn choose an envelope and place each "egg" into his side of the carton. You take a turn next. Choose an envelope and place each "egg" into your side of the carton. The first to have one egg in each hole gets a special treat.

One, Two, Three

SUBJECT: Mathematics/Counting

LEVEL: 3 years old

PURPOSE: Develop the concept of rational counting to three
Reinforcing colors and shapes

MATERIALS: Attribute blocks

PROCEDURE Allow the child to choose three blocks. Have her recite the number names with you if necessary. Ask the child how many blocks she has. Ask appropriate questions of the child: "How many are blue? How many are circle shapes? How many are large?" etc.

Match 'em

SUBJECT:	Mathematics/Geometry
LEVEL:	4 years old
PURPOSE:	Practice identifying plane figures
MATERIALS:	Various shapes (and sizes) cut from thick paper (i.e., oak tag) A bulletin board on which the shapes have been traced
PROCEDURE:	Have the child choose a shape and match it with its outline. Hang it on the bulletin board.

Squares and Triangles

SUBJECT:	Mathematics/Geometry
LEVEL:	4 years old
PURPOSE:	Practice naming plane shapes: square, triangle
MATERIALS:	Square and triangle shapes from the attribute blocks
PROCEDURE:	Allow the child to sort the blocks into two piles according to shape. Discuss differences. Identify by name. For reinforcement, put a few blocks into a paper bag or feel box. Allow the child to feel a block and attempt to identify it by name.
VARIATION:	As the child becomes familiar with the shapes, more may be included.

Snack Time

SUBJECT:	Mathematics/Ordering
LEVEL:	3 years old
PURPOSE:	Teach understanding of concepts of more and less

MATERIALS: Small snacks such as raisins

PROCEDURE: During snack time, set up two rows of raisins (Fig. 10-19). Allow the child to choose one row. Reinforce words with comments such as, "Sandy, you must really like raisins. You picked the row that has more. This row has less."

Kitchen Helpers

SUBJECT: Mathematics/Sorting

LEVEL: 3 years old

PURPOSE: Provide experience in directed sorting

MATERIALS: Silverware
Drawer organizer with indentations shaped for the utensils (available in most variety stores)

PROCEDURE: Briefly discuss the shapes of the indentations. Ask the child to sort accordingly.

Larger, Smaller

SUBJECT: Mathematics/Sorting

LEVEL: 3 years old

PURPOSE: Provide practice in directed sorting
Teach proper use of longer, shorter

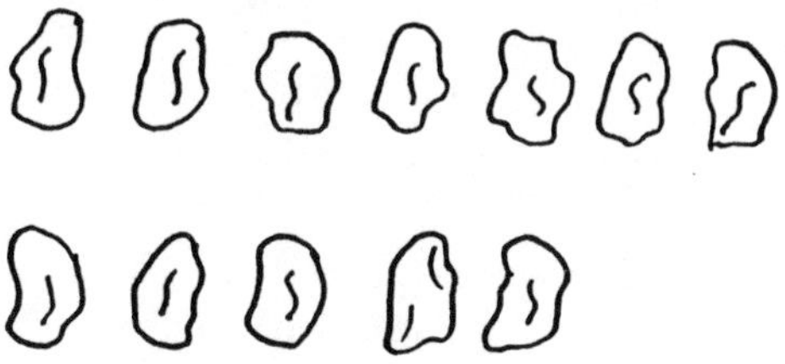

Figure 10-19

MATERIALS: Building blocks of same shape but of two sizes
             Two cardboard cartons or boxes

PROCEDURE: Direct the child to put all of the shorter blocks in one
             box and the larger ones in the other box.

What's Alike, What's Different?

SUBJECT: Mathematics/Sorting

LEVEL: 3 years old

PURPOSE: Help children notice likenesses and differences

MATERIALS: From around the house collect items which are alike in
             one way yet different in another, such as two blocks,
             same shape, different size; a crayon and a pencil; a coat
             and a sweater; toy truck and doll; banana and apple;
             pictures of a horse and a dog.

PROCEDURE: Show two of the items. Ask the child how the items are
             alike and how they are different.

ADAPTATION: Show two pairs of items. Ask children to choose the
             one from the second pair that belongs with the pair you
             are holding.

Baking Cookies

SUBJECT: Mathematics/Geometry

LEVEL: 3 and 4 years old

PURPOSE: Reinforce knowledge of plane shapes

MATERIALS: Premixed cookie dough
             Cookie cutters in the shapes being reinforced
             Oven

PROCEDURE: Allow the child to press the dough into the cookie
             cutters. After baking, the child will enjoy "eating the
             shape."

Mobiles

SUBJECT:	Mathematics/Geometry
LEVEL:	3 and 4 years old
PURPOSE:	Reinforce the child's knowledge of plane shapes
MATERIALS:	Yarn or shoelaces Separators (cut from straws) Various triangle, square, rectangle, and circle shapes cut from construction paper Hanger
PROCEDURE:	Have the child string shapes to make a colorful mobile. Tie strings to hanger (Fig. 10-20).

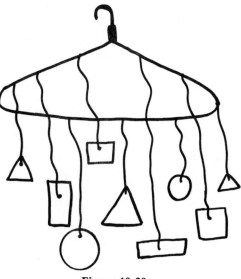

Figure 10-20

Pictures from Shapes

SUBJECT:	Mathematics/Geometry
LEVEL:	3 and 4 years old
PURPOSE:	Reinforce knowledge of plane shapes
MATERIALS:	Circle, square, rectangle, triangle shapes
PROCEDURE:	Allow children to compose a picture using the shapes (Figs. 10-21 to 10-24).

What Next?

SUBJECT:	Mathematics/Ordering
LEVEL:	3 and 4 years old
PURPOSE:	Develop understanding of ordering by time sequence
MATERIALS:	Picture cards in sets of three: bird building nest, nest with eggs, bird feeding baby bird; plant sprouting, with

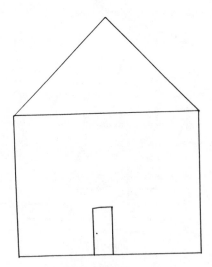

Figure 10-21

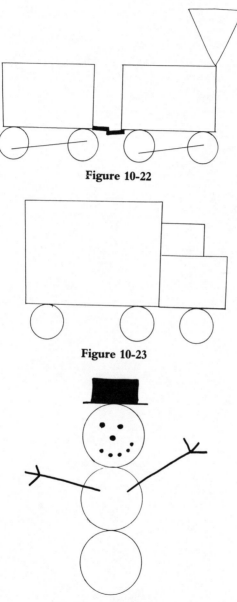

Figure 10-22

Figure 10-23

Figure 10-24

leaves, with flower; wrapped gift, child removing wrapping, child lifting toy; double-dip ice cream cone, single dip, almost finished

PROCEDURE: Have the child arrange the pictures in the correct order (Figs. 10-25 and 10-26).

Finger Painting

SUBJECT: Mathematics/Geometry

LEVEL: 3, 4, and 5 years old

PURPOSE: Reinforce the concept of plane shapes

MATERIALS: Finger paint
Patterns made by cutting bottom from a milk container (square), small cereal box (rectangle), juice can (circle), and the corner of a shoe box (triangle)

PROCEDURE: Allow the child to make designs by dipping shapes into paint and pressing on paper.

Number Book

SUBJECT: Mathematics/Ordering

LEVEL: 3, 4, and 5 years old

Figure 10-25

Figure 10-26

PURPOSE: Encourage development of counting objects

MATERIALS: Construction paper
Old magazines
Crayons
Scissors
Glue

PROCEDURE: See the activity, "Make Your Own Book: Variations" (p. 77).

The Three Bears

SUBJECT: Mathematics/Ordering

LEVEL: 3, 4, and 5 years old

PURPOSE: Develop listening skills
Develop ability to order by size and to transfer order to other set

MATERIALS: Mounted illustrations from the *Three Bears*
Flannel board (To make a flannel board: glue felt to same-size poster board)

PROCEDURE: As the child listens to the story, have her keep a picture record of the order of events, matching the chairs, bowls, and beds with the appropriate bears. Then have the child recount the story using the pictures as a guide.

Community Helpers

SUBJECT:	Mathematics/Classification
LEVEL:	4 years old
PURPOSE:	Teach children to identify the tool used by each worker
MATERIALS:	Pictures of men and women in various occupations: carpenter, farmer, doctor, plumber, etc. The child can help collect these from old magazines. Picture cards each depicting a tool used by one of the workers.
PROCEDURE:	Have the child match the tool to the worker.

What Is It For?

SUBJECT:	Mathematics/Classification
LEVEL:	4 years old
PURPOSE:	Teach children to identify items by use
MATERIALS:	A set of picture cards of things to ride in; things to wear; things to eat; things that give light; things to feed pets; building tools; garden tools. *To make picture cards:* use pictures from old magazines. Cut out appropriate pictures. Glue picture to a 3 x 5 index card. Cover with contact paper for protection.
PROCEDURE:	Have the child sort the cards into the appropriate piles. An adaptation of "Go Fish" can be played by dealing two, four, or five cards to each player. Take turns asking for cards in a particular category.

Dominoes I

SUBJECT:	Mathematics/Counting
LEVEL:	4 years old
PURPOSE:	Develop concept of rational counting to six

MATERIALS: Large cardboard dominoes constructed by placing the dots in different positions

PROCEDURE: Place dominoes face down on the floor. Have the child select six dominoes. You do the same. Have the child place one domino in the center of the circle. You must match either side of the domino (Fig. 10-27). If you do not have a match, you must draw from the pack until one is found. The first one to use all of their dominoes gets a special treat.

Guess How Many?

SUBJECT: Mathematics/Counting

LEVEL: 4 years old

PURPOSE: Develop concept of rational counting to five

MATERIALS: Feel box or cloth
Small objects

PROCEDURE: Place two to five similar objects into the feel box (or under a cloth). Ask the child to identify by feeling the type and number of objects.

Stringing Beads

SUBJECT: Mathematics/Ordering

LEVEL: 4 years old

PURPOSE: Teach children to duplicate a pattern

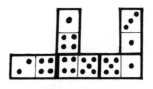

Figure 10-27

MATERIALS: Wooden beads
               Yarn or shoelaces for stringing
               Picture cards with patterns for stringing beads

PROCEDURE: Ask the child to duplicate the pattern you have drawn
               (Fig. 10-28). Some possibilities, arranged in order of
               difficulty: red, yellow, red, yellow . . . ; cube, cube,
               sphere, cube, cube, sphere . . . ; small, larger, largest,
               small, larger, largest . . . ; green, blue, red, red, green,
               blue, red, red . . . ; yellow, green, yellow, blue, yellow,
               red . . . ; cube, sphere, cube, sphere, sphere, cube,
               sphere, sphere, sphere . . .

VARIATIONS: Use pegs on a pegboard to form patterns
               Use stickers on paper

Buttons

SUBJECT: Mathematics/Sorting

LEVEL: 4 years old

PURPOSE: Directed sorting
               Reinforcing colors

MATERIALS: Many assorted buttons
               Lengths of yarn threaded into blunt needles

PROCEDURE: Have the child string the buttons by color

VARIATION: Have the child string the buttons by size

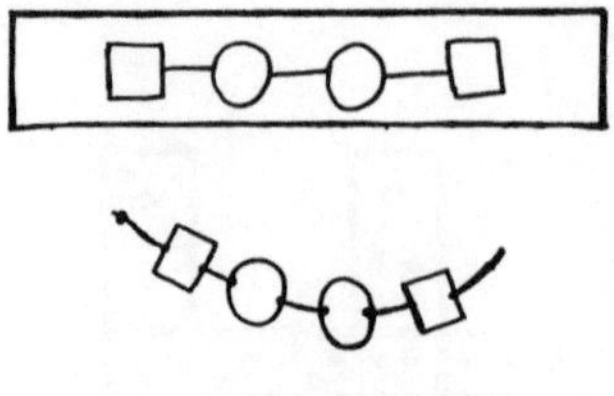

Figure 10-27

Autumn Leaves

SUBJECT: Mathematics/Sorting

LEVEL: 4 years old

PURPOSE: Practice directed sorting

MATERIALS: Many colored leaves collected during an Autumn Na-
ture Walk (see the activity, "Things of Nature," p. 181)
Paper
Glue

PROCEDURE: After the nature walk, ask the child to find the leaves
that might have grown on the same tree. Shape is the
only consideration. The child will need to disregard
color and size. Arrange a colorful display and glue the
leaves on the paper.

Sorting Box Activities

SUBJECT: Mathematics/Sorting

LEVEL: 4 years old

PURPOSE: Practice directed sorting

MATERIALS: A sorting box. This is easily made by cutting slits into
the lid of a shoe box. A strip of oak tag is folded to form
the separators.
     Materials to be sorted: geometric shapes; picture
cards of things we eat, wear, play with (if you don't
have any, cut out pictures from magazines, tape or glue
them to an index card and cover with contact paper for
protection); picture cards of birds, fish, mammals; holiday pictures—things relating to Halloween, Thanks-
giving, Valentine's Day (holiday stickers on index cards
are quite satisfactory)

PROCEDURE: Have child sort according to directions. After sorting,
the child can remove the lid to check if the items in
each section are alike (Figs. 10-29 and 10-30).

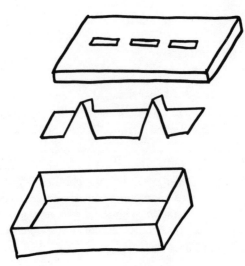

Figure 10-29

Figure 10-30

Undirected Sorting

SUBJECT: Mathematics/Sorting

LEVEL: 4 years old

PURPOSE: Develop the ability to recognize similarities

MATERIALS: A box of beads and blocks
An empty box

PROCEDURE: Ask the child to "straighten these out." If the child does not see the implication, return to directed sorting.

VARIATIONS: 1. Attribute blocks with directions: "Put the ones together that belong together."
2. Collection of nails, screws, washers, say, "Fix these the way they belong."
3. Box of assorted crayons

Multiple Sorting

SUBJECT: Mathematics/Sorting

LEVEL: 4 years old

PURPOSE: Develop the ability to sort according to two properties

MATERIALS: Attribute blocks

PROCEDURE: First, ask the child to sort by color. Next, have each of these subjects sorted by shape (or size or thickness).

Which One Doesn't Belong?

SUBJECT: Mathematics/Classification

LEVEL: 4 and 5 years old

PURPOSE: Determine if a child is able to reverse her thinking and see a situation from another point of view

MATERIALS: Sets of three objects with two possible groupings such as a lead pencil, a red pencil, a red crayon; pictures of a dog, a goldfish, a squirrel; pictures of a sled, a wagon, an automobile; pictures of an ice cream cone, a sandwich, a dish of ice cream; pictures of a fishing pole, a fish, a frog

Attribute blocks: small red triangle, small blue triangle, large red triangle; two baby dolls, boy and girl, one adult doll; cup, saucer, drinking glass; pictures of a child wearing glasses, adult wearing glasses, child without glasses.

PROCEDURE: The dialogue might be as follows:

PARENT: Look at these things on the table. We are going to play a guessing game. I think that one of these doesn't go with the others. Pick up the one that doesn't belong.

CHILD: I know. It's this. (She holds up the crayon.) Those are pencils and this is a crayon.

PARENT: That is a very good idea. (Return the crayon to the table.) I have a different idea. (Choose the lead pencil.)

CHILD: That's not right. That's a pencil and this is a pencil and this is a crayon.

PARENT: You picked the crayon but I could be right, too. The pencil I picked isn't red like these are.

The comment you make shows that you have reached a flexibility of thought beyond that of the child. The ability to reverse opinions that are based on sensory imagery shows a higher form of reasoning, according to Piaget. The child is not being willfully stubborn; she simply is unable to accept a viewpoint other than her own. More docile children may appear to be "learning" by agreeing with your verbal explanation, but further questioning might reveal no real understanding.

For the next set of objects, you go first. Have the child

go second to see if she can find another possible solution. Continue to guide her as needed.

Guess What I Am

SUBJECT:	Mathematics/Classification
LEVEL:	4 and 5 years old
PURPOSE:	Teach the child to identify an object by the sound it makes
MATERIALS:	Picture cards of things that make identifiable sounds, such as a dog, a train, a cow, a baby, a fly. Children may enjoy finding their own pictures in old magazines.
PROCEDURE:	Have the child begin by choosing a card and holding it so you cannot see it. He then makes the appropriate sound and you need to try and guess the object. When you get it right, it is your turn to make the noise and the child's turn to guess what the object it.

Farm Fun

SUBJECT:	Mathematics/Geometry
LEVEL:	4 and 5 years old
PURPOSE:	Reinforce the concepts of inside, outside, on
MATERIALS:	A bulletin board or flannel board showing a farm yard with a barn and a fence forming a corral Pictures of farm animals *To make a flannel board*, you need poster board, glue, and felt large enough to cover poster board. Glue the felt onto the poster board to cover entire area. *For pictures to stick to the flannel board:* glue small pieces of sandpaper or Velcro to the back of the pictures.
PROCEDURE:	Have the child put the cow IN the barn, the chicken ON the fence, the horse INSIDE the corral, and so on.

VARIATION: Make a gate on the fence, a door on the barn. When the
              gate is closed, the dog is inside; when the gate is
              opened, since the dog is now free, there is no longer an
              "inside."

Find a Shape

SUBJECT: Mathematics/Geometry

LEVEL: 4 and 5 years old

PURPOSE: Foster awareness of shapes

MATERIALS: Various geometric solids (many of these are in a set of
            blocks) (Figs. 10-31 and 10-32).

PROCEDURE: Choose a block and discuss its shape. Ask: "Does it
            have any 'points' (vertices)? How many? How many
            flat surfaces (faces)? What are the shapes of the faces?
            Can you count the edges?" Allow the child to handle
            the block. Next, ask her to find a "shape like this" in the
            room. As objects are identified, similarities and differ-
            ences are discussed.

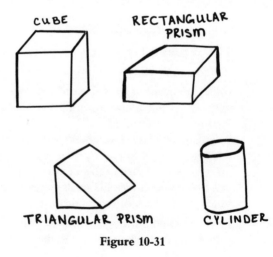

Figure 10-31

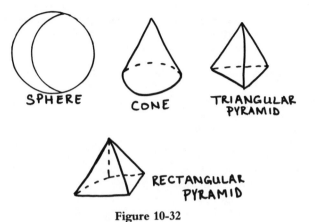

Figure 10-32

VARIATION: Using the same blocks, ask the child to recall some-
             thing that is shaped the same as something she has at
             home, sees when she goes outside, or when she is with
             you at the store, etc.

Lots of Birthdays

SUBJECT: Mathematics/Ordering

LEVEL: 4 and 5 years old

PURPOSE: Practice ordering by the number of elements and trans-
             ferring order to another set

MATERIALS: Pictures of five birthday cakes
             Pictures of children from 1 to 5 years old

PROCEDURE: Explain that today is the birthday of each of the chil-
             dren in the pictures, and that each has his or her own
             cake. Have the child draw one candle on a cake, one
             more on the next cake, and so on. Mix up the pictures
             and have them rearranged on the "one more than"
             principle. Finally, have the child match each picture of

a child with the cake that has the correct amount of candles.

Some or All?

SUBJECT:	Mathematics/Classification
LEVEL:	5 years old
PURPOSE:	Check on understanding of the terms "some" and "all"
MATERIALS:	4 red triangles 1 blue triangle 3 blue squares (Attribute blocks may be used or the figures could be cut from construction paper)
PROCEDURE:	After allowing children to view the figures and discuss them, ask, "Are all of the triangles red? Are all of the blue ones squares?"

Bulletin Display

SUBJECT:	Mathematics/Numerals
LEVEL:	5 years old
PURPOSE:	Teach the child to associate numerals with sets
MATERIALS:	Chart with numerals (ribbons attached) and sets in random order
PROCEDURE:	Have the child match each numeral to a set (Fig. 10-33).

Clothespin Soldiers

SUBJECT:	Mathematics/Numerals
LEVEL:	5 years old
PURPOSE:	Learn sequencing of the numerals

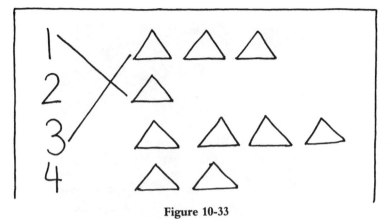

Figure 10-33

MATERIALS:	"Soldiers" made by sketching a face and a numeral on a wooden clothespin (Fig. 10-34)
PROCEDURE:	Have the child arrange "soldiers" in order on a line.
VARIATION:	You'll need a chair and a jug. Place the jug behind the chair. Have the child kneel on the chair (Fig. 10-35). See if you and the child can drop the "soldiers" in the jug in numerical order.

Coloring Numerals

SUBJECT:	Mathematics/Numerals
LEVEL:	5 years old

Figure 10-34

Figure 10-35

PURPOSE: Develop numeral writing readiness
             Practice reading numerals and following directions

MATERIALS: Numeral sheets
             Crayons

PROCEDURE: Tell the child to follow your directions, then say, "Color the five green" (Fig. 10-36).

Figure 10-36

VARIATION: You'll need tissue paper and glue. Have the child take
              small pieces of tissue paper and crumble them into
              little balls with their fingers (develops fine motor
              skills). Glue tissue paper balls to the numerals follow-
              ing the direction of which the numeral is written (Fig.
              10-37).

Dominoes II

SUBJECT: Mathematics/Numerals

LEVEL: 5 years old

PURPOSE: Help the child associate the numerals with sets

MATERIALS: Dominoes with set of dots on one half, a numeral on
              the other

PROCEDURE: Have the child match the dot side to a numeral side.
              Take turns with the child.

Figure 10-37

Find a Pair

SUBJECT: Mathematics/Numerals

LEVEL: 5 years old

PURPOSE: Develop association between numerals and sets

MATERIALS: Make a playing deck using 21 3 x 5 cards. Ten contain the numerals 0 through 9. Ten show sets of 0 to 9 elements. One is the lucky card.

PROCEDURE: Deal all cards. Have the child draw a card from you and put down all of his pairs. Continue in like manner. The player holding the lucky card after all of the pairs are found gets a special treat.

Find the Numerals

SUBJECT: Mathematics/Numerals

LEVEL: 5 years old

PURPOSE: Practice numeral writing readiness

MATERIALS: Duplicate simple pictures containing "hidden" numerals (Fig. 10-38)

PROCEDURE: Have the child trace over the numerals.

Find Your Name

SUBJECT: Mathematics/Numerals

LEVEL: 5 years old

Figure 10-38

PURPOSE: Practice reading numerals

MATERIALS: Numeral cards displayed around the room

PROCEDURE: Give the child a numeral name, then ask them to find
the numeral and pick it up. Continue until all the cards
are found. Numeral cards may be hidden to add interest.

Find Your Partner

SUBJECT: Mathematics/Numerals

LEVEL: 5 years old

PURPOSE: Practice matching like numerals

MATERIALS: Two sets of numeral cards

PROCEDURE: Place the cards face down. Take turns flipping over
cards to find a match. When you find a match, go again.
If you do not find a match, turn both cards face down
and the next player takes a turn. Person with most
matches gets a special treat.

Go Fish

SUBJECT: Mathematics/Numerals

LEVEL: 5 years old

PURPOSE: Enhance numeral recognition

MATERIALS: Deck of playing cards (face cards may be removed)

PROCEDURE: Give each player seven cards, which are held or placed
out of view of other player(s). Place the rest of the deck
face down in the center. A player begins by asking the
person on her left for a card that will match one in her
hand. If the second player has the card, she must give
it up. If she does not, she says, "Go Fish." The first
player draws from the deck until she finds a match.
When all four cards of any number are collected, they

are placed on the table. The first person to run out of cards gets a treat.

VARIATION: The card game "War" reinforces the less than and greater than relationships.

Match the Numeral

SUBJECT: Mathematics/Numerals

LEVEL: 5 years old

PURPOSE: Practice matching like numerals

MATERIALS: Two sets of numeral cards

PROCEDURE: Deal one set of numeral cards out until all are gone. Leave the other set of numeral cards in a pile face down. Turn one card over at a time. The person holding the match card holds it up, takes the matching card to make a set. First person to run out of cards gets a treat.

My Number Book •

SUBJECT: Mathematics/Numerals

LEVEL: 5 years old

PURPOSE: Make a counting, numeral activity

MATERIALS: Construction paper
             Loose-leaf binder rings

PROCEDURE: Have the child prepare a booklet containing numerals he has written associated with appropriate sets.

Number Train

SUBJECT: Mathematics/Numerals

LEVEL: 5 years old

PURPOSE: Develop association of numerals with sets

MATERIALS: Pictures of an engine and boxcars
Small pictures to fill each car

PROCEDURE: Have the child number each boxcar in order and place the appropriate number of items in it. As each new numeral is learned, another car is added.

Numeral-Go-Round

SUBJECT: Mathematics/Numerals

LEVEL: 5 years old

PURPOSE: Practice matching like numerals

MATERIALS: A circular-shaped cardboard with the numerals 1 through 9
Clip clothespins with the numerals printed on them

PROCEDURE: Have the child clip the clothespins to the chart matching the numerals (Fig. 10-39).

Figure 10-39

Numeral Puzzles

SUBJECT: Mathematics/Numerals

LEVEL: 5 years old

PURPOSE: Help the child learn to associate the numeral to a set

MATERIALS: Set of puzzles with numerals and sets (these are available commercially or may be made) (Fig. 10-40).

PROCEDURE: Have the child match the numeral to the set. These puzzles are self-correcting.

Practice before Paper

SUBJECT: Mathematics/Numerals

LEVEL: 5 years old

PURPOSE: Practice numeral writing—unhappy results disappear quickly!

MATERIALS: Container (frozen vegetable box is a convenient size) filled with sand or salt (Fig. 10-41), or "Magic Slate" or chalkboard

PROCEDURE: Allow the child to practice writing in sand or salt or on "Magic Slate" or chalkboard before attempting more permanent results.

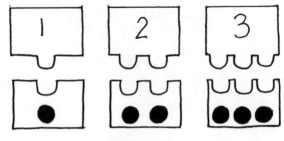

Figure 10-40

Figure 10-41

Sorting Box

SUBJECT: Mathematics/Numerals

LEVEL: 5 years old

PURPOSE: Practice matching like numerals

MATERIALS: Sorting box labeled with numerals (Fig. 10-42)
Pack of numeral cards

PROCEDURE: Have the child sort the cards by matching numerals.
Cards for which there are no matches may be placed in
a separate pile.

Stencils

SUBJECT: Mathematics/Numerals

LEVEL: 5 years old

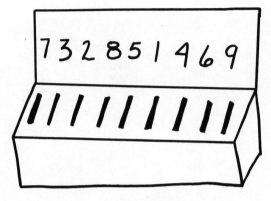

Figure 10-42

PURPOSE:	Develop numeral writing readiness
MATERIALS:	Numeral stencils
PROCEDURE:	Have the child trace through the stencil (Fig. 10-43).

Sticker Fun

SUBJECT:	Mathematics/Numerals
LEVEL:	5 years old

Figure 10-43

PURPOSE: Teach the child to associate numerals with sets

MATERIALS: Numeral sheet for each player
Stickers
Spinner

PROCEDURE: Have the child begin by spinning the spinner and reading the numeral to which it points. She counts out the
correct number of stickers and pastes them next to the
numeral on her card (Fig. 10-44). The first one to
complete her card gets a special treat.

Twister

SUBJECT: Mathematics/Numerals

LEVEL: 5 years old

PURPOSE: Practice sequencing of the numerals

MATERIALS: Large numeral cards

PROCEDURE: Place the numeral cards on the floor at random. Have
the child step on them in order.

VARIATIONS: 1. Have the child step on them as you call each number.

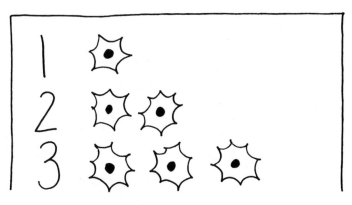

Figure 10-44

2. Use cards with shapes. Have the child step on the shape you call out.
3. Use cards with colors. Have the child step on the color you call out.

Grid Game

SUBJECT:	Mathematics/Ordering
LEVEL:	5 years old
PURPOSE:	Develop the ability to follow directions involving position: left, right; top, middle, bottom
MATERIALS:	A grid containing nine squares, three across and three down, for each child Nine different stickers for each player
PROCEDURE:	Have the child place stickers according to your directions: "Find you blue star and put it in the bottom, left corner." Point to the top left corner. "Paste your red heart there." Continue until each position is filled (Fig. 10-45).

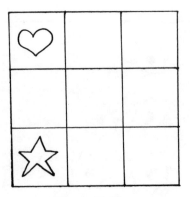

Figure 10-45

Seasons

SUBJECT:	Mathematics/Ordering
LEVEL:	5 years old
PURPOSE:	Introduce repeating order
MATERIALS:	Pictures of seasonal activities that the child has found in old magazines Bulletin board
PROCEDURE:	Discuss with the child the four seasons of the year. Have the child sort the pictures into sets for each season. Display on the bulletin board in clockwise order, with the current season on the top. Reinforce through discussion, stressing that season follows season, year after year.

Who Sits Where?

SUBJECT:	Mathematics/Ordering
LEVEL:	5 years old
PURPOSE:	Practice ordering according to the number of elements
MATERIALS:	Pictures (from a catalog) of tables with from zero to eight chairs
PROCEDURE:	• Say to the child, "Pretend that we are going to get a new set of table and chairs. Which do you think would be good for our family? Remember that each person needs a chair." Allow the child to make a choice and to tell who would sit in each chair.
	• Now say, "There is one picture that doesn't have any chairs. Let's put that first. Which do you think we should put next?" Continue ordering in like manner. Counting may be reinforced by naming the number of chairs in order.

Computer

SUBJECT: Mathematics/Readiness for addition

LEVEL: 5 years old

PURPOSE: Practice reading numerals
             Readiness for addition

MATERIALS: Large box for a child to sit in with an "input" slit and
             on "output" window cut into the front (Fig. 10-46)
             "Input" cards with sets of dots
             Numeral cards for "output"

PROCEDURE: Give the child (the "computer") the numeral cards.
             Insert two input cards. After making appropriate
             noises, the computer (the child) shows the numeral
             card that names the sum.

Fish

SUBJECT: Mathematics/Readiness for addition

LEVEL: 5 years old

PURPOSE: Practice union of sets
             Addition readiness

Figure 10-46

MATERIALS: Bag of fish crackers
One piece of blue paper for each player ("ocean")

PROCEDURE: Place "ocean" on the table. Place from one to five fish on each paper and explain that today will be a "five-fish day." Ask the child to tell how many more fish he needs to make five. Next, direct the child to move the fish about while you ask questions, for example: "Two fish swim to the top of the ocean while the rest swim to the bottom. How many are on the bottom? One more swims to the top. Now how many are on the top? All except one fish dives to the bottom and along comes a great big fish (the child) and gobbles up the one on the top. How many fish are left?" The activity continues until all the fish are eaten.

VARIATION: Animal crackers in a circus cage

Going Fishing

SUBJECT: Mathematics/Readiness for addition

LEVEL: 5 years old

PURPOSE: Practice addition readiness

MATERIALS: A large box lid for the fish pond
A fishing pole with a magnet for a hook
Many cardboard fish with paper clip mouths on which two sets of different colored spots have been drawn (Fig. 10-47)

PROCEDURE: Show the child how to "catch" a fish with the magnet. Ask her to count the spots on the fish she "catches" and then count the total number of spots. If the child counts correctly, let her keep the fish.

Make a Set

SUBJECT: Mathematics/Readiness for addition

LEVEL: 5 years old

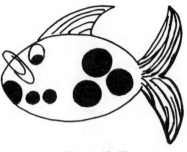

Figure 10-47

PURPOSE: Practice numeral recognition, counting, joining sets

MATERIALS: Set of uniformly sized blocks
            One block with the numerals one to six on the faces

PROCEDURE: Have the child toss the block, read the numeral, count
            out the appropriate number of blocks, and place them
            in a line. He then throws again, placing the second set
            of blocks with the first and counts to find the total. You
            do the same thing and place your blocks under the first
            set. The player with the most blocks keeps all of the
            blocks; the player with the most blocks at the end of the
            game gets a special treat.

Matho

SUBJECT: Mathematics/Readiness for addition

LEVEL: 5 years old

PURPOSE: Practice addition readiness

MATERIALS: Player cards on which the numerals being practiced
            have been written (Fig. 10-48)
            Caller cards, folded in half, with appropriate set of dots
            on the outside (Fig. 10-49)

PROCEDURE: Draw a caller card and show one side to the child. Have
            the child count the dots and then show her the other

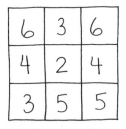

Figure 10-48

side of the card. Ask the child to cover the numeral which names the sum. Continue until all numbers on her card are covered.

Touch and Find

SUBJECT:	Mathematics/Sorting
LEVEL:	5 years old
PURPOSE:	Practice sorting, using the sense of touch
MATERIALS:	Feel box Children's clothing—hat, mitten, sweater, scarf
PROCEDURE:	Have the child find an article in the box that you describe, by saying, for example, "Find something to wear on your head. Fine something you should have two of," and so on.
VARIATIONS:	1. Use swatches of fabric: smooth, rough, furry. 2. Attribute blocks—find two that have the same shape.

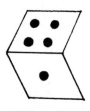

Figure 10-49

Which Ones Go Together?

SUBJECT: Mathematics/Sorting

LEVEL: 5 years old

PURPOSE: Practice undirected sorting
            Notice if a child can form his own sorting plan

MATERIALS: Set of animal picture cards including farm animals,
            pets, circus animals. (If you do not have these, you can
            cut out pictures from old magazines, glue them on
            index cards, and cover with contact paper for protec-
            tion.)

PROCEDURE: Tell the child, "Put these in piles the way you think
            they belong." Assist the child as needed.

VARIATIONS: Use pictures of foods ordinarily eaten at breakfast,
            lunch, and dinner; pictures of children doing seasonal
            activities; pictures of things that give light, make noise,
            move.

Science (2–5 Years Old)

Collage of Nature

SUBJECT: Science

LEVEL: 2 years old and up

PURPOSE: Learn about different objects of nature
            Creativity with different things of nature
            Develop small muscle ability

MATERIALS: Leaves, pine cones, acorns, grass, small sticks, flowers
            and other objects found outside
            Large piece of paper
            Glue

PROCEDURE: Place a large piece of paper down flat. The floor may be
            a good place to work. Lay out all the different items you
            have collected from outside. Spread glue around and

have the child put the items on the paper where there is glue. Allow him to create as he wishes. Assist if needed. Join in the creation to give encouragement to the child.

NOTE: This is a follow-up to the activity, "Things of Nature" (p. 181).

Outline of My Body

SUBJECT: Science

LEVEL: 3 years old and up

PURPOSE: Body awareness

MATERIALS: Large piece of paper (longer and wider than the child)
Crayons, markers, or colored pencils
Strands of yarn
Glue

PROCEDURE: • Roll paper out flat on the floor. Have the child lay down on the paper. Outline the child's body with writing instrument (Fig. 10-50). Have the child stand up and look at the outline of her body.
• Cut out the child's body outline with her assistance (Fig. 10-51). Lay outline of body onto the floor. Give the child the yarn, glue, and writing instruments. Tell the child to draw the face, glue on hair, and color the body as she wants herself to look. When completed, hang it up somewhere for everyone to see.

NOTE: This can be used as a follow-up activity to "Catch My Shadow" (pp. 183–184).

Silhouette

SUBJECT: Science

LEVEL: 3 years old and up

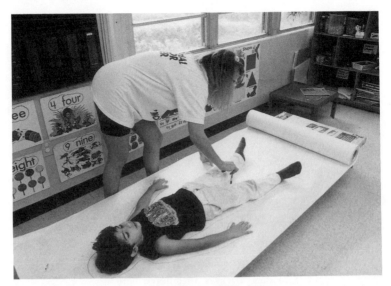

Figure 10-50

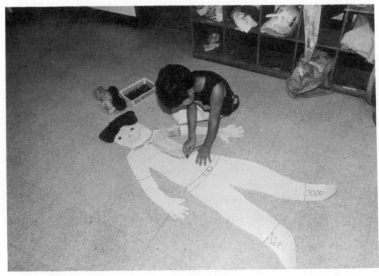

Figure 10-51

PURPOSE: Demonstrate how objects in front of a light in the darkness cause shadows

MATERIALS: Film projector or flashlight
Dark room
Black paper
Chalk
White paper
Scissors

PROCEDURE: • Bring the child into a dark room with the light from the flashlight or film projector on. Shine the light on wall nearby. Hold your hand in front of the light to demonstrate the shadow your hand makes (Fig. 10-52). Make different movements with your fingers. Let the child do it.

Figure 10-52

- Tape the black sheet of paper on the wall at the same level as the child's head. Shine the light on the paper. Have the child stand in front of the light sideways (so eyes are not in the light). Trace the child's shadow with chalk (Fig. 10-53).
- Return to a lighted room. Cut silhouette out with scissors. Glue the silhouette to the white paper. Write the child's name, date, and age on it as a keepsake. Hang it up for display (Fig. 10-54).

NOTE: This is a great follow-up activity for "Catch My Shadow" (pp. 183–184).

Revolution

SUBJECT: Science

LEVEL: 4 and 5 years old

Figure 10-53

Figure 10-54

PURPOSE: Learn how the earth revolves around the sun while turning slowly round and round
Coordination

MATERIALS: Apple (Earth)
Grapefruit (Sun)

PROCEDURE: *Part I:* Tell the child that the yellow grapefruit is the sun and the apple is the earth. The earth is where we live. The earth rotates round and round, causing day and night. Demonstrate:

1. Have the child hold the sun (grapefruit). Mark a spot on the apple as the place that you live. Hold the apple near the sun with the spot you marked facing the sun.
2. Tell the child, "Now it is daytime and the sun is shining on us." Point to spot on apple that is marked (Fig. 10-55).

Figure 10-55

3. Slowly turn the apple and tell the child, "Now it is nighttime as we turn away from the sun." Point to the spot on the apple that is marked (Fig. 10-56). Then tell the child, "This is what causes daytime light hours and nighttime dark hours."

4. Switch parts. Allow the child to be the earth and you be the sun.

Part II: Tell the child, "While the earth turns around in a circle, it also rotates around the sun. This makes the days, weeks, months, and year complete." Demonstrate:

1. Have the child return to being the sun and you be the earth. Continue to turn the earth in your hand. Begin to slowly walk around the child. Tell the child that this is called "revolu-

Figure 10-56

tion" (Figs. 10-57 and 10-58). Tell him, "It takes one year for the earth to make a complete circle around the sun. Everytime you have a birthday, the earth has made a circle around the sun. It takes a long time."
2. Switch positions. You be the sun and allow the child to be the earth. Assist the child as needed.

NOTE: An activity to go along with this one is "The Earth Goes Round and Round" (pp. 185–186).

Self-Help Skills (1–5 Years Old)

Mealtime

SUBJECT: Self-help skills

Figure 10-57

Figure 10-58

LEVEL: 1 year old

PURPOSE: Develop ability to finger feed self

MATERIALS: Highchair with tray *or*
Small table and chair (the child should be comfortably seated with elbows just above the table surface)

PROCEDURE: Start by putting a small amount of finger food on the child's tray. See if she will pick it up and eat. Praise her for eating by herself if she can do this. If the child does not attempt to pick up the food and eat it or just simply plays with it, follow these steps for teaching self-feeding:

1. Demonstrate finger food eating yourself.
2. Gently take the child's hand and assist her to:
   a. pick up the food
   b. lift it to her mouth
   c. put food in her mouth
   d. put hand down on table
3. Repeat steps several times. Be sure food is completely gone from child's mouth before beginning the next bite.
4. Gradually decrease assistance by eliminating one step at a time.
5. After child has successfully completed each step, decrease praise. Eating should be rewarding in itself.

On the Potty

SUBJECT: Self-help skills

LEVEL: 1 1/2 years old

PURPOSE: To teach child to use the potty (toilet) when taken by an adult

MATERIALS: Potty chair

PROCEDURE: The child may not fully indicate that he would like to use the potty. The responsibility to follow through falls on the adult. Take the child frequently and consistently to establish a regular schedule. Recommended times to take the child would be after drinking and eating, after naps, and after playing hard.

Praise the child for cooperating and/or performing. Make a big deal over the child performing so that he becomes more aware of what he is supposed to do when he is seated on the potty chair. Show the child what he has done and praise him.

If the child doesn't perform immediately after sitting and you feel it is a good time for having the child remain on the potty chair for possible performance, read a story to the child or involve him in listening activities so that he will sit longer.

Continue the process until child is successful.

NOTE: The child will still soil her pants at this age and may not always perform when you want him to. Be patient and make sure to praise the child when his performance is successful. Treat accidents lightly.

Eating with a Spoon

SUBJECT: Self-help skills

LEVEL: 2 years old

PURPOSE: Develop ability to feed self with a spoon held with a fist

MATERIALS: Dish with sides (and suction cup on bottom)
Food (in small bite-sized pieces or soft foods, i.e., mashed potatoes)
Spoon

PROCEDURE: Take the child's hand and hold it over the spoon handle. Tell the child it's time to eat. Help the child get some food onto her spoon and into her mouth.

Next time, let go of the child's hand before it reaches her mouth. Then let go of it when she is further away from her mouth. Continue to do less each time until the child is doing it successfully by herself.

Buttons and Snaps

SUBJECT: Self-help skills

LEVEL: 3 years old and up

PURPOSE: Develop ability to unbutton front buttons and fasten large, front snaps
Develop fine motor ability

MATERIALS: Buttoning board (Fig. 10-59)
Snap board (Fig. 10-60) (can be commercially bought in school supply stores or be made at home)

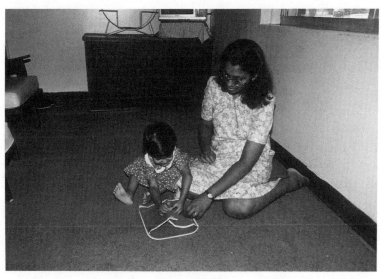

Figure 10-59

Figure 10-60

To make a buttoning board: Staple or nail a partial shirt front to a board. Sew on buttons beginning with very large ones on top and decrease in size as you go down. Be sure to cut button holes to fit each button.

PROCEDURE: Unbuttoning: While the child is watching, unbutton all but one button. Ask the child to unbutton the last button. If it is necessary, partially unbutton each button and allow the child to finish the task. Allow him to start with the largest button first.

Snaps: Demonstrate to the child how you fasten a snap. Be sure the child has enough strength to squeeze a snap together. If he has trouble, help him practice on other things that must be squeezed, i.e., pinch-type clothespin. Show the child how to position the top half of the snap over the bottom half, grasping the snap with fingers over one side and the thumb under the other, and squeezing it together. Slowly snap all the snaps but one. Have your child do the last one. Next time, you do one and have the child do the rest. Assist the child as needed.

NOTE: Toy stores sell "Dress My Dolls," which also aid in learning unbuttoning and fastening snaps (i.e., Ernie, Mickey Mouse) (Fig. 10-61).

Pouring the Beverage

SUBJECT: Self-help skills

LEVEL: 3 years old

PURPOSE: Develop ability to pour liquid from a small pitcher into a cup

MATERIALS: 2-cup pitcher
Cup
Beverage

Figure 10-61

PROCEDURE: • As a start, whenever the child would like something
to drink, allow the child to pour the beverage with
your direct assistance. Stand directly behind the
child. Have your left hand go over her left hand and
your right hand over her right hand. Have her right
hand pick up the pitcher and the left hand hold the
cup. With your assistance have the child pour the
beverage into the cup to fill it half way (Fig. 10-62).
When you say "stop," set the pitcher upright on the
table.

Figure 10-62

- Begin to let go of her hand just as you say "stop." Allow the child to turn the pitcher upright unassisted. Gradually decrease the amount of assistance you give the child.

Writing Skills (1–5 Years Old)

The Beginning Writer

SUBJECT: Writing skills

LEVEL: 1 year old and up

PURPOSE: Expose the child to writing tools and paper
Encourage writing

MATERIALS: Pencil and paper to start. Later allow the child to experiment with other writing tools such as markers, colored pencils, crayons, felt-tip pens

PROCEDURE:
- While the child is watching, hold pencil and write on the paper. Give the child a pencil by holding it out in front of him. Let him choose the hand he would like to use. Tell him to write on the paper. Praise the child for writing on the paper.
- Later, when you expose the child to other writing tools, allow the child to make choices of which one he prefers. Watch him create. Display the child's pictures around the house.

A Mess of Fun

SUBJECT: Writing skills

LEVEL: 1 1/2 years old and up

PURPOSE: Prewriting experience
Cause and effect

MATERIALS: Whipped cream, shaving cream, or finger paints

Table
Smock or old shirt
Newspaper or old cloth for the floor

PROCEDURE: Push up the child's sleeves and put a smock or old shirt on her. Spray shaving cream on table in front of the child. Tell the child to put her hands in it and have fun. Join in with the child and demonstrate different motions with the child such as making circles with your hands, drawing and writing with your fingers.

NOTE: As the child approaches 2 1/2 years old, she will start using her whole hand while finger painting. At 3 1/2, she may finger paint using her fingers and whole hand. At about 4 years old, the child may finger paint using fingers, hands, and arms.

Lines and Circles

SUBJECT: Writing skills

LEVEL: 2 years old

PURPOSE: Teach the child beginning writing skills after demonstrating

MATERIALS: Paper and pencil

PROCEDURE:
- Demonstrate a vertical line to the child. Hold pencil in front of the child, allowing him to take it with preferred hand. Tell the child to do it. Hold his hand and help him do it if necessary. Reinforce action with praise. Repeat process until child can do it alone.
- Demonstrate a horizontal line to the child. Follow same procedure as above.
- Demonstrate the "V" stroke to the child. Follow same procedure as above.
- Demonstrate the circular stroke. Follow same procedure as above.

Build a House of Shapes

SUBJECT: Writing skills

LEVEL: 5 years old

PURPOSE: Draw a simple house utilizing familiar shapes

MATERIALS: Paper and pencil

PROCEDURE: Demonstrate to the child the following, step by step, and allow the child to repeat each step immediately after you:

1. Start with a large square.
2. Peak the square off with a large triangle to make a roof (Fig. 10-63A).
3. Draw another large square connected to the first square (Fig. 10-63B).
4. Draw small squares for windows.
5. Draw a small rectangle for a door with a little circle for the doorknob.
6. Draw a very small rectangle for a garage door handle (Fig. 10-63C).
7. Draw a long rectangle along side of house to make a chimney. Add smoke if you like (Fig. 10-64).

There's your house. Add some trees, clouds, birds, the sun, flowers to the scene if you like.

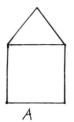 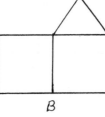 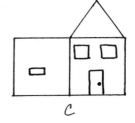

Figure 10-63

Figure 10-64

Copy Your Name

SUBJECT:	Writing skills
LEVEL:	5 years old
PURPOSE:	Practice copying first name when shown name printed on paper
MATERIALS:	5 x 7 index cards
	Pencil
PROCEDURE:	• Print the child's name (first letter capitalized, other letters lowercase) on two separate 5 x 7 index cards. Cut one of the cards between each letter. Show the other card to the child. Have the child match the cut letters to the completed index card with her name on it. Assist the child as needed.
	• Give the child a 5 x 7 index card and pencil. Hold pencil in front of the child to allow her to pick it up with preferred hand. Tell the child to write her name on the card just like she sees it already written.
NOTE:	The child's letters may be large, irregular, or reversed when writing. This is normal for this age. At approximately 5 1/2 years old, the child may begin to write her name without a model. Letters may be irregular or reversed.

Chapter 11

Activities in the Park

INTRODUCTION

Outdoor activities enable children to learn about the outside world, develop their gross motor skills (large muscles), and allow them to express themselves freely. The activities in this chapter will help children in these areas along with several other developmental subject areas.

The physical development of children occurs very quickly; therefore, it is important to give them an opportunity for outdoor experiences. Being outdoors gives children the proper environment to do things that are not always acceptable or possible to do indoors. Often, the outdoors offers children space to explore and do exciting things loudly with no restrictions.

Here are some ideas for utilizing things around you while at the park:

1. Jungle gyms are great for dramatic play. With a little imagination, they can become a fire engine, an airplane, or even a spaceship.

Children often can get up on the jungle gym by themselves but are afraid to come down. Encourage the child to climb down instead of being lifted down. In helping the child climb down, have her turn around and back down. Guide her feet to the rungs and give reassurance and the feeling that she did it by herself.

2. Sand or the sandbox and a few plastic items can reinforce the concepts of measuring and full/empty. When there is wet sand, have the child wear old clothing. Provide shovels, cookie cutters, molds, and plastic containers. The child can make mud pies, castles, and more.

3. Give the child a bag to collect things while on a nature walk. Have the child listen for and identify the sounds around him. Encourage him to feel various textures, such as tree bark, sand, grass, rocks. Discuss how these things feel.

Have fun with the following activities and remember it is especially important to provide close and careful supervision for the children while they are outdoors.

ACTIVITIES

Creative Exploration (3–5 Years Old)

Hide and Seek

SUBJECT: Creative exploration

LEVEL: 3 years old and up

PURPOSE: Develop problem-solving skills
Develop ability to look beyond the obvious

MATERIALS: Any objects familiar to the child

PROCEDURE: First show the child the object you are going to hide. Have the child hide her eyes and you hide the object. Tell the child that she needs to find the object you hid. Use signals such as "cold" for far away, "warm" for getting close to it, and "hot" for it's right there. Teach the child these signals before she starts to look. As the child begins to look for the object, use the signals and remind her what each means. Then let her hide the object and you find it.

VARIATIONS: Easter Egg Hunt. Hide eggs and have the child look for
              them.
              Hide yourself and have the child find you. Let her hide
              and you try to find her.

Gross Motor Skills (1–5 Years Old)

Flying through the Sky

SUBJECT: Gross motor development

LEVEL: 1 year old and up

PURPOSE: Develop gross motor ability (large muscles)
              Provide experiences using the imagination

MATERIALS: None

PROCEDURE: Pretend to be an airplane. Extend your arms straight
              out to each side. Run through the park making the
              sound of an airplane. Pretend to take off and land (be
              careful not to crash).

Push Me– Pull Me

SUBJECT: Gross motor skills

LEVEL: 1 1/2 years old

PURPOSE: Develop ability to push or pull large lightweight objects
              Develop balance and coordination

MATERIALS: Baby doll stroller (baby doll to put in stroller—op-
              tional)
              Wagon (put toys in it—optional)

PROCEDURE: • Demonstrate to the child how to push the stroller.
                Tell the child to "push" the stroller. Encourage him
                to take his baby for a walk.
              • Demonstrate to the child how to pull a wagon. Tell
                the child to "pull" the wagon. Encourage him to put
                toys in it.

Kick Ball

SUBJECT: Gross motor skills

LEVEL: 1 1/2 years old and up

PURPOSE: Develop ability to kick a ball while standing still without support
Practice balance and coordination

MATERIALS: Beach ball or other lightweight ball

PROCEDURE: While the child is watching, demonstrate kicking the ball while standing still without support. Have the child try it. If the child needs help, kneel next to her, lift her foot, and help her foot kick the ball. Work with the child until she kicks the ball by herself. As the child grows bigger and stronger, heavier balls can be used. As the child approaches 5 years old and her ability to run and kick improves, encourage her to walk up and kick the ball.

VARIATION: When the child masters kicking the ball without assistance, kick the ball back and forth to each other.

Hopping Down the Trail

SUBJECT: Gross motor skills

LEVEL: 2 years old and up

PURPOSE: Develop ability to jump with two feet onto a designated spot

MATERIALS: Chalk or strips of material

PROCEDURE: Mark a spot with an "X" (can use chalk or material). Follow this progression as skills develop:

1. Jump in place with two feet off the ground.
2. Jump forward to designated spot with two feet off the ground.
3. Specify a trail. Hop like a bunny following the trail. Demonstrate each step to the child before

having him try it. Children need visual examples and should be assisted as needed.

The Backward Walk

SUBJECT: Gross motor skill

LEVEL: 2 1/2 years old

PURPOSE: Develop ability to walk backward
Practice balance and coordination

MATERIALS: None

PROCEDURE: In a safe, obstacle-free environment, demonstrate how to walk backward to the child. Have the child walk backward slowly while holding your hand as you walk with her. Allow the child to do it on her own after she is walking steadily.

VARIATION: After child successfully walks backward, encourage her to pull a wagon while walking backward.

Catch the Ball

SUBJECT: Gross motor skills

LEVEL: 3 years old and up

PURPOSE: Catch ball with extended arms

MATERIALS: Plastic or foam rubber 5-inch ball

PROCEDURE: Start close to child. Toss ball lightly in the air toward the child, telling him to catch it. Repeat it several times. Gradually move farther away, up to 3 feet.

VARIATIONS: Use beanbags and pillows

Chalk Walk

SUBJECT: Gross motor skills

LEVEL: 3 years old and up

PURPOSE: Develop balance

MATERIALS: Chalk

PROCEDURE: Make zigzag lines with chalk on concrete. Have the child follow the line, walking with one foot in front of the other. Demonstrate for the child first. Encourage her to use her arms for balance.

Overhand Throw

SUBJECT: Gross motor skills

LEVEL: 3 years old and up

PURPOSE: Develop ability to throw ball overhand

MATERIALS: Whiffle ball

PROCEDURE: While the child is watching, throw the ball overhand. Tell the child that you just threw the ball overhand. Do it one more time for the child to observe. Now tell him, "You try it. Throw the ball overhand as far as you can." Work with the child until he is comfortable with it.

Goals: throw a distance of 5 feet at 3 years of age; throw the ball 10 feet at 4 years of age.

Ride That Tricycle

SUBJECT: Gross motor skills

LEVEL: 3 and 4 years old

PURPOSE: Develop ability to ride a tricycle

MATERIALS: Tricycle

PROCEDURE: • Have the child sit on the tricycle. Push her slowly to get a feel for how the tricycle works.
• Place the child's feet on the pedals. Push her feet on the pedals to make them go around (Fig. 11-1).
• Tell the child to push with her legs. If necessary, push on your child's knees until she can do it on her

Figure 11-1

own. Push the child to keep her going. Gradually decrease the distance you push her to eventually allow her to go alone.

- You will probably need to start her off for awhile. Then allow her to get herself started on the tricycle.

Goals: 3 years old—on level ground and around wide corners; 4 years old—around obstacles and sharp corners.

VARIATIONS: Allow the child to use other wheeled toys, i.e., big wheel, fire truck, tractor.

Follow That Shape

SUBJECT: Gross motor skills/Mathematics

LEVEL: 4 years old

PURPOSE: Develop ability to walk lines of different shapes without stepping off the line
Foster awareness of shapes (geometry)

MATERIALS: Chalk (on concrete) or rope (on grass)

PROCEDURE:
- Make large shapes—circle, triangle, square, heart, and/or rectangle.
- Have the child name the shapes if he can. Help him as needed.
- Tell the child that you want him to follow the lines of the shape that you name. "Jimmy, walk the lines of the triangle."
- If he doesn't know which shape is the triangle, show him. While he walks the lines of the triangle, talk about the triangle. Get the child "acquainted" with each shape as he walks it.
- After he finishes walking the lines of the shape, ask the child what shape it is. Assist as needed.

Giddyap Horsey

SUBJECT: Gross motor skills

LEVEL: 4 years old

PURPOSE: Develop ability to skip on one foot or gallop

MATERIALS: None

PROCEDURE:
- Demonstrate by hopping on one foot slowly and stepping with the other.
- Take one hop forward with the child. Step with the other foot forward to almost meet the first. Put it together: "hop—step" (Figs. 11-2 and 11-3).
- Gradually increase speed.
- Pretend to be a horse and "giddyap."

Figure 11-2

Figure 11-3

Hopscotch

SUBJECT: Gross motor skills

LEVEL: 4 years old

PURPOSE: Develop ability to hop on one foot
             Eye–hand coordination
             Balance

MATERIALS: Chalk
             Sidewalk, cement, or concrete
             Stones

PROCEDURE: • Draw a hopscotch diagram on the sidewalk (Fig.
             11-4). Give the child a stone. Have her drop it on the
             first block. Tell her to stand on one foot and bend
             over to pick up her stone. If done successfully, have
             her go to the next number, hop on one foot to
             number one, and pick up her stone from number
             two (Fig. 11-5).

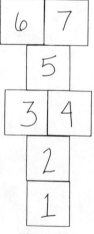

Figure 11-4

Figure 11-5

- Continue on in order of numbers. If child is unsuccessful with any of the numbers, leave stone where last successful number was completed. Now you take a turn.

Jump Over Those Sharks

SUBJECT:	Gross motor skills
LEVEL:	4 years old
PURPOSE:	Develop ability to run and jump over line for distance of 2 feet
MATERIALS:	Tape or pieces of material Pictures of sharks
PROCEDURE:	Place tape down at 6, 12, 18, and 24 inches. Put pictures of sharks in between each line. Have the child jump

from line to line over the sharks. Gradually work child up to jumping full distance of 2 feet.

Hang in There

SUBJECT: Gross motor skills

LEVEL: 4 1/2 years old

PURPOSE: Develop ability to hang from overhead bar parallel to the ground using an overhand grip with feet off the ground

MATERIALS: Overhead bar parallel to the ground

PROCEDURE: Demonstrate to the child how to hang from the overhead bar using an overhand grip with your feet off the ground. Have the child put his hands on the bar with an overhand grip. Hold the child until he has a tight grip. Before letting go of him, let him know that you're letting go. Have him hold on for as long as he can, aiming to reach a goal of holding on for 5 seconds. Encourage the child to gradually increase the time he supports his weight.

Activity Dice

SUBJECT: Gross motor skills

LEVEL: 4 and 5 years old

PURPOSE: Develop large muscles
                Develop ability to follow directions
                Learn number concepts

MATERIALS: • One large die with room for an activity on each side. Use square box. Cover with construction paper. With permanent marker, write down an activity (jump, spin around, flap like a bird) on each side of the box (Fig. 11-6).

Figure 11-6

- One large die with a number on each side. *To make:* same as above, but instead of writing an activity, write a number on each side (Fig. 11-7).

PROCEDURE:
- Have the child throw the activity die. Read the activity that lands face up. Then have the child throw the number die. Read the number of times the child must do that activity. If the child can read numbers, allow the child to read the numbers.
- Now you take a turn. Have the child count with you while you are doing the activity specified.

Figure 11-7

It's Hula Hoop Time

SUBJECT:	Gross motor skills
LEVEL:	4 and 5 years old
PURPOSE:	Develop large muscle ability
	Coordination
MATERIALS:	Hula hoop
PROCEDURE:	Take a hula hoop and demonstrate to the child how to use it by putting it around your waist, spinning your hips round and round. Give it to the child to try (Fig. 11-8). After some practice, it should become easier for

Figure 11-8

her to do. It's a challenge to see if you can keep the hula hoop going round and round. Give the child praise for her attempts as well as for succeeding in this great venture.

NOTE: As the child progresses, she can try using two or three hula hoops at one time.

Up on a Beam

SUBJECT: Gross motor development/Balance

LEVEL: 4 and 5 years old

PURPOSE: Develop gross motor ability (large muscle)
Practice balance

MATERIALS: Log or other object sturdy enough to stand and walk on

PROCEDURE: Demonstrate balance for the child by walking on the log, extending your arms straight out to your sides. Allow the child to try it by first holding one of his hands. When he is ready, let him try it without holding on to you at all.

CAUTION: Always walk along side the child, prepared to catch him in case of falling.

Skipping Along

SUBJECT: Gross motor skills

LEVEL: 5 years old

PURPOSE: Develop ability to skip alternating with each foot

MATERIALS: None

PROCEDURE:
• Demonstrate how to skip, alternating with each foot. Have the child do it slowly while you say "step-hop, switch, step-hop, switch, step-hop . . . " (Figs. 11-9 and 11-10).
• Start slowly. Practice until the child can do it smoothly. Gradually increase speed.

Figure 11-9

Figure 11-10

Language Development (2–5 Years Old)

Colors Around You

SUBJECT: Language development/Defining colors

LEVEL: 2 years old and up

PURPOSE: Learn colors and develop awareness of colors around the child
Strengthen visual awareness

MATERIALS: None

PROCEDURE: Look around you. Point to different things and ask the child what color it is. If she does not know, tell her. Any color that is being learned for the first time can be reinforced by finding many things with that color.

Listen Around You

SUBJECT: Language development/Auditory discrimination

LEVEL: 2 years old and up

PURPOSE: Develop listening skills
Learn to discriminate between loud and quiet sounds

MATERIALS: None

PROCEDURE: Sit down or walk around the park very quietly and listen to what you hear around you. In a quiet voice tell each other what you hear (whisper). Teach the child which noises are loud and which are quiet. Allow the child to tell you which are loud and which are quiet.

Fire Engine, Fire Engine

SUBJECT: Language development/Safety

LEVEL: 2 years and up

PURPOSE: Develop listening skills and recall
Learn about fire safety

MATERIALS: Write down the following verse on a piece of paper so you remember it:

> The fire engine goes "woo, woo, woo."
> The horn goes "beep, beep, beep."
> And the fireman says, "You better hurry up,
> so we can put the fire out!"

PROCEDURE: While you are at the park you may hear sirens blow or a fire truck go by. This would be a great time to teach your child this verse, as well as any other time. Follow this procedure to help the child learn it:

Tell the child: "Listen first and then repeat what I say with me."

Say: "The fire engine goes woo, woo, woo."
Then have the child repeat it with you.

Say: "The horn goes beep, beep, beep."
Have the child repeat it with you.

Say: "The fireman says, 'You better hurry up.' "
Have the child repeat it with you.

Say: "so we can put the fire out!"
Have the child repeat it.

NOTE: As the child becomes more and more familiar with the words, he will sing the song with you, instead of repeating it line by line.

Feel Around You

SUBJECT: Language development/Tactile discrimination

LEVEL: 2 years old and up

PURPOSE: Discriminate between hard and soft, rough and smooth
Provide experience for language development

MATERIALS: None

PROCEDURE: Walk around the park. Feel things that you see. Allow the child to feel things. Talk about each thing you feel. Teach the child which objects are hard and soft, rough and smooth.

CAUTION: Be sure the things you feel are safe. Do not allow your child to feel anything that will hurt her.

VARIATION: Gather some safe objects to touch. Have the child close her eyes and guess what she is feeling. Have her tell you if it is hard or soft, rough or smooth.

Identify Object by Use

SUBJECT: Language development

LEVEL: 2 1/2 years old

PURPOSE: Develop ability to identify objects by use

MATERIALS: Common objects, e.g., ball, shoes, sliding board

PROCEDURE: Keep in mind that the child learns from what is surrounding him and what is said to him. The child needs many hands-on experiences with everyday things and the language to go along with these experiences. Practice explaining to the child what he is doing during daily routine activities and encourage the child to say the following:

> "Your shoes go on your feet."
> "A ball can be thrown or kicked."
> "You slide down the sliding board sitting on your bottom."

Name That Action

SUBJECT: Language development

LEVEL: 2 1/2 years old

PURPOSE: Develop ability to identify common actions

MATERIALS: None

PROCEDURE: Children need to be exposed to concrete experiences involving actions and names for these actions. Help the child to describe her actions throughout your daily routine of activities. It is an important language builder.

> "You are running on the grass."
> "Patti is riding her bicycle."
> "Daddy threw the ball far."

Teach the child action words as she performs them. Name an action for the child to perform. Demonstrate if needed.

Follow Me

SUBJECT: Language development/Gross motor development

LEVEL: 3 years and up

PURPOSE: Provide opportunity for learning how to follow directions and imitate
Develop language skills
Develop gross motor ability (large muscles)

MATERIALS: None

PROCEDURE: Explain to the child that you are going to be the leader. Tell him to watch you and do whatever you do or say whatever you say. Give the child a chance to be the leader.

NOTE: While at the park you can develop your child's gross motor skills by utilizing space to walk, run, hop, etc.

Put the Fire Out

SUBJECT: Language development/Gross motor skills

LEVEL: 3 years old and up

PURPOSE: Develop language

Develop large muscle ability
Opportunity for dramatic play

MATERIALS: Cardboard tube from wrapping paper

PROCEDURE:
- It's time to use some imagination with the jungle gym. Pretend it's a firetruck. You and the child are on your way to a fire. Make the noise of sirens. Make the sound of a horn blowing and a bell ringing. Encourage your child to join in with all the sound effects.
- Upon arrival at the fire, quickly get out of the fire truck. Have the child get her hose (cardboard tube) and start spraying the fire out. Use your imagination to add to this activity. Allow the child to improvise.

What Begins with the Letter . . . ?

SUBJECT: Language development

LEVEL: 4 and 5 years old

PURPOSE: Teach letter sounds
Develop language skills

MATERIALS: None

PROCEDURE: Pick a letter for the day. Teach the child the name of the letter and the sound it makes. Look for objects around you that begin with that letter. Help the child to find things. Allow the child to find things on his own. Give guidance as needed.

NOTE: You will find an activity that can be used along with this one in Chapter 10 called "Make Your Own Book" (pp. 75–77). This is also a fun activity to do in the car.

Story in the Sky

SUBJECT: Language development/Imagination

LEVEL: 4 and 5 years old

PURPOSE: Develop language skills
            Encourage the child to use her imagination
            Encourage freedom of expression

MATERIALS: Clouds in the sky
            Blanket (optional, to lie down on)

PROCEDURE: • Lie down on your back and look up at the sky. Tell
              your child to look at the clouds and the different
              shapes they make. Sometimes they look like people
              or things we see around us.
            • Tell the child what things you see that the clouds are
              shaped like. Give the child a turn.
            • Try to make a story with what you see. Anything
              goes with your imagination.

NOTE: You will find a follow-up activity in Chapter 10 called
            "Puffy Clouds" (pp. 70–71).

I Know My Senses

SUBJECT: Language development

LEVEL: 5 years old

PURPOSE: Develop ability to identify use of senses

MATERIALS: None

PROCEDURE: Teach the child the following (point to each part of
            your body as you say it):

                    I see with my eyes—LOOK
                        Look, see the clouds in the sky.
                    I hear with my ears—LISTEN
                        Listen, hear the birds singing.
                    I smell with my nose—BREATHE
                        Breathe in, smell the pretty flowers.
                    I taste with my mouth—TASTE
                        Eat and taste the delicious pizza.
                    I touch with my hands—FEEL
                        Feel the soft, cute puppy.

Mathematics (3–5 Years Old)

Follow the Leader

SUBJECT:	Mathematics/Ordering
LEVEL:	3 years old
PURPOSE:	Teach words of position: over, under, through
MATERIALS:	Set up an obstacle course using large boxes, and/or playground equipment
PROCEDURE:	Give directions to the leader. As children follow, they call out their position: over the box, under the bar, through the tunnel.

Move About

SUBJECT:	Mathematics/Ordering
LEVEL:	4 years old
PURPOSE:	Develop the ability to feel a pattern using large muscle coordination
MATERIALS:	None
PROCEDURE:	Have the child repeat and continue patterns, such as two jumps, one clap, twirl about; one step in, one jump, one step out, clap above your head.
VARIATION:	Tape an 8-foot line on the floor using electrician's tape for durability. Do not label the line with numerals. Have the child follow your pattern. Example: one step, one jump, two steps, one jump, three steps, etc.

Roll and Jump

SUBJECT:	Mathematics/Counting
LEVEL:	4 and 5 years old
PURPOSE:	Practice rational counting

MATERIALS: One die

PROCEDURE: Designate a starting point and a finishing line. Take turns rolling the die and take the appropriate number of jumps. The first to cross the finish line gets a treat.

Pebbles of Different Sizes

SUBJECT: Mathematics/Ordering

LEVEL: 4 and 5 years old

PURPOSE: Learn math concepts such as ordering, counting, adding, and subtracting
                  Develop fine motor ability (small muscles)

MATERIALS: Pebbles, stones, rocks of various sizes

PROCEDURE: First collect pebbles, stones, and/or rocks of various sizes. Have the child arrange them in order from biggest to smallest.

VARIATIONS: Count the pebbles (3 years and up)
                  Adding and subtracting (5 years old): Use pebbles in small groups to add, i.e., two pebbles combined with three pebbles is how many pebbles? Use a small group of pebbles to subtract, i.e., five pebbles take away two pebbles is how many pebbles?

Personal–Social Skills (3 1/2–5 Years Old)

May I Play with This?

SUBJECT: Personal–social skills

LEVEL: 3 1/2 years old and up

PURPOSE: Ask permission to use items belonging to others, rather than just taking them

MATERIALS: None

PROCEDURE: When other children are playing at the park, and have things to play with that are not your child's, teach him to ask if he can play with it before he takes it. For example: Your child and another child are playing in the sandbox. Your child would like to use the shovel that belongs to the other child. Teach your child to ask if he can use that shovel before picking it up and using it. Be sure to praise him when he asks for it. This will reinforce the desired behavior.

Prewriting Skills (4–5 Years Old)

Stick in the Mud

SUBJECT:	Prewriting skills/will vary depending on what the child is writing or drawing (see *Variations*)
LEVEL:	4 and 5 years old
PURPOSE:	Develop writing skills Develop fine motor ability (small muscle)
MATERIALS:	Stick and dirt or sand
PROCEDURE:	Use the stick to write or draw various things in the dirt or sand. See *Variations* for ideas.
VARIATIONS:	• *Shapes:* circle, square, triangle, heart, rectangle (math, 4 and 5 years old) • *Numerals:* from one to nine (math, 5 years old) • *Letters, words* (language, 5 years old) • *Pictures* (art, 4 and 5 years old)
NOTE:	A reinforcement activity to go along with this one is "Make Your Own Book," pp. 75–77.

Science (1–5 Years Old)

Sandy Experience

SUBJECT:	Science/Sand
LEVEL:	1 year old and up

PURPOSE: Provide the child with a tactile and visual experience

MATERIALS: Coarse sand (sandblasting sand is perfect—about $2.00 per 10 lb)
Bucket and shovel
Funnel
Toy colander
Trucks, tractors, etc.

PROCEDURE:
- Allow the child to sit in sand and feel it with her hands. Take off your child's shoes and socks and allow her to walk in it and curl her toes in it.
- Provide *necessary* guidance, using the shovel to fill the bucket with sand. Turn it upside down and lift off the bucket slowly to make a castle. Allow the child to crush the castle with her hands and feet if she desires. Allow the child to use the funnel and colanders in the sand. She can see how it comes through the hole(s). Play with the trucks and tractors in the sand. Make hills and have the trucks drive over them.

Splish, Splash

SUBJECT: Science/Water

LEVEL: 1 year and up

PURPOSE: Experience the natural enjoyment of water play

MATERIALS: Container (i.e., basin) of water, or small, shallow pool filled ankle-deep with water
Towel
Extra set of clothing (optional)
Plastic measuring cups
Small pitchers
Funnel
Washable baby dolls

PROCEDURE:
- Allow the child to experience the water. Let him sit in the pool, get wet, splash it with his hands. Pour

small amounts over his shoulders, arms, and legs while in the pool.

- Demonstrate the use of other objects in the water such as measuring cups, funnels, etc. Allow the child to experience using the objects. Let the child give the baby doll a bath.

CAUTION: Always provide close supervision when the child is playing around any amount of water.

VARIATIONS: Add liquid detergent and food color to container of water (Fig. 11-11). Do not put liquid detergent in pool. Teach the child the name of the color that you use.

Evaporation

SUBJECT: Science

LEVEL: 2 years old and up

Figure 11-11

PURPOSE: Observe how water disappears from a concrete area on a sunny day

MATERIALS: A sunny day
             Water
             Paintbrush

PROCEDURE: Allow the child to paint with water on the sidewalk or any concrete area. Tell her to watch it disappear. Tell her the sun is hot and drys the water from the sidewalk. "The sun makes the water disappear." You can tell your older child that this is called evaporation. "The sun soaks up all the water and it makes a cloud in the sky. When that cloud gets too full of water, it rains."

Tiny Bubbles

SUBJECT: Science/Bubbles

LEVEL: 2 years and up

PURPOSE: Experience visually how soapy liquid can make bubbles
             Develop breath control

MATERIALS: Bottle of bubbles and a small wand.
             • *To make your own bubbles:* use small amount of liquid detergent, water, and glycerin or sugar.
             • *To make your own wand:* Make an enclosed circle at one end of a pipe cleaner; use the other end of pipe cleaner as the handle.

PROCEDURE: Show child how to make bubbles by dipping the wand into the liquid bubble solution and blowing on it gently or swishing the wand gently through the air. Allow your child to try it.

VARIATIONS: Catch the bubbles and watch them disappear (eye–hand coordination; cause and effect)
             Count the bubbles (match/counting)

Things of Nature

SUBJECT:	Science/Nature
LEVEL:	2 years and up
PURPOSE:	Explore and learn about the objects of nature
MATERIALS:	Things around you at the park Big bag to put things in
PROCEDURE:	Take the child around the park and gather different things of nature (e.g., sticks, leaves, etc.). Explain to the child what each thing is and that they are part of nature.
NOTE:	Take the things you collected home with you to do some activities. (See "Collage of Nature," pp. 134–135 and "Autumn Leaves," p. 109).

Where Does Rain Come From?

SUBJECT:	Science/Evaporation
LEVEL:	4 and 5 years old
PURPOSE:	Learn about evaporation and "where rain comes from"
MATERIALS:	None
PROCEDURE:	While looking at clouds, tell the child: "Rain comes from clouds. The sun pulls up water from the ground and makes big clouds. When the clouds get real full, rain comes down. Then the cycle starts all over again."

Rub-A-Dub-Dub

SUBJECT:	Science/Friction
LEVEL:	4 and 5 years old
PURPOSE:	Learn what friction is and experience how it works
MATERIALS:	Write down the following verse on a piece of paper so you have it with you:

Friction. What is friction?
Friction is a rub-a-dub-dub, rub-a-dub
of objects that are moving
in a rub-a-dub-dub, rub-a-dub
of friction at work.

PROCEDURE: Tell the child: "Friction is a rubbing together of objects that are moving." Rub your hands together and say "rub-a-dub-dub." Have the child do it. Continue to rub your hands together and recite the following in a singsong fashion:

Friction. What is friction?
Friction is a rub-a-dub-dub, rub-a-dub
of objects that are moving
in a rub-a-dub-dub, rub-a-dub
of friction at work.

Teach the child to sing the words with you.

What Goes Up, Must Come Down

SUBJECT: Science/Gravity
LEVEL: 4 and 5 years old
PURPOSE: Learn about gravity
             Develop gross motor ability (large muscle)
MATERIALS: Ball
PROCEDURE: • Tell the child: "Gravity is what keeps us down on the ground instead of floating away."
             • Jump up in the air. Tell the child that it was gravity that pushed you back down.
             • Tell the child to jump. Tell the child gravity brought him back down.
             • Take the ball and throw it straight up in the air and watch it come down. Tell the child that gravity did

it again. It made the ball come back down. Whatever goes up, comes back down.
- Let the child throw the ball up in the air.

Up, Up, and Away

SUBJECT: Science/Helium

LEVEL: 4 and 5 years old

PURPOSE: To demonstrate how helium works

MATERIALS: Two helium-filled balloons

PROCEDURE:
- On your way to the park, stop at a party store. Purchase two helium balloons to take with you. Request a salesperson to fill up the balloons in front of you for your child to see. Explain to the child: "They are using a special air called helium to fill up the balloon. Helium causes the balloon to fly away. You need to hold onto it tight." Tie the balloon loosely around your child's wrist. You take charge of the other balloon.
- When you are at the park say to the child, "You saw at the store how they filled the balloons. They used a special air called helium. Helium makes the balloon fly away. I'll give you the balloon I have and say 'ready, set, go,' and you let go of the balloon. Then we'll both say 'up, up, and away.'" When you're ready, begin.

Catch My Shadow

SUBJECT: Science/Light and darkness

LEVEL: 4 and 5 years old

PURPOSE: Demonstrate how objects between the sun and the ground cause shadows

Develop coordination and gross motor ability (large muscle)

MATERIALS: Sunlight

PROCEDURE: • Tell the child that the sun causes light. Objects block the light and cause shadows. Point out your shadows to the child. Show her the shadows from the trees and other things around you.
              • Step on the child's shadow. Have the child step on your shadow. Now, start the chase to see who can get the other person's shadow. Take turns chasing each other's shadow (Fig. 11-12).

NOTE: Follow-up activities are "Outline of My Body" (p. 135) and "Silhouette" (pp. 135–138).

Figure 11-12

The Earth Goes Round and Round

SUBJECT: Science/Revolution

LEVEL: 4 and 5 years old

PURPOSE: Demonstrate the concept of revolution
            Develop gross motor ability (large muscle)

MATERIALS: None

PROCEDURE: • Explain to the child: "We live on a great big round
              ball called the earth. It turns very slowly, going
              round and round and makes a circle around the
              sun."

Figure 11-13

- Pretend to be the earth and turn round and round. Have the child pretend to be the sun. Spin around slowly (like the earth) while making a circle around the child (the sun) (Fig. 11-13). Then switch positions.

NOTE: A follow-up activity is "Revolution" (pp. 138–142).

Let's Go Fly a Kite

SUBJECT: Science

LEVEL: 5 years old

PURPOSE: Experience flying a kite
Learn how wind carries light objects
Develop gross (large) and fine (small) motor abilities
Develop coordination

MATERIALS: Kite

PROCEDURE:
- Find a wide open area. Explain to the child that when the wind blows on something very light, like a kite, it causes it to blow away.
- Demonstrate this to the child by flying the kite. Give the child an opportunity to hold the kite while it is flying in the air.

Chapter 12

Activities in the Car

INTRODUCTION

Most children tend to feel confined when riding in a car because they have nowhere to run, walk, or even move about. Within the car itself, there is not much stimuli to keep a child entertained. For this reason, parents should encourage their child to look out the windows and notice things along the road. There are so many beautiful things in nature to see and learn about. The sky is the limit. Teach the child about such things as the clouds and rain. Sing songs to keep the child entertained.

Implement the following activities to amuse the children while developing their skills. Some of the activities can be carried out by using things within your vehicle. Materials needed are listed for each activity. Other activities involve noticing the outside surroundings while you are driving along.

ACTIVITIES

Fine Motor Skills (1–5 Years Old)

Playing the Spoons

SUBJECT: Fine motor skills

LEVEL: 1 year old

PURPOSE: Develop eye–hand coordination
            Develop rhythm

MATERIALS: 2 spoons (not plastic)

PROCEDURE: • Place one spoon in each hand of the child. Make
              sure she has a grip on the spoons.
            • Demonstrate beating two spoons together to the
              child.
            • Tell her it is her turn. Immediately reinforce the
              child's actions by cheering when she successfully
              beats the spoons together.
            • Turn on the radio for her to play the spoons to the
              music.

My Hand

SUBJECT: Fine motor skills

LEVEL: 3 years old

PURPOSE: Develop ability to wiggle thumb and fingers individ-
            ually while other fingers are closed into a fist

MATERIALS: None

PROCEDURE: Sing the following song with the child to the tune of
            "Are You Sleeping":

> Where is thumbkin? (wiggle thumb, right hand)
> Where is thumbkin?
> Here I am! (wiggle thumb, left hand)
> Here I am!
> How are you today, sir? (wiggle thumb, right
>   hand)
> Very well, I thank you. (wiggle thumb, left hand)
> Run away. (move right hand behind your back)
> Run away. (move left hand behind your back)

Repeat the verse by substituting "pointer," "tall man,"
"ring man," and "pinky" for "thumbkin" to represent
the other fingers.

Pinch a One . . .

SUBJECT: Fine motor skills

LEVEL: 4 and 5 years old

PURPOSE: Develop ability to grasp with finger and thumb
Develop coordination in hand
Muscle control

MATERIALS: None

PROCEDURE: Demonstrate spreading fingers wide with your palm facing the child. While the child is watching, touch your thumb with the tip of each finger beginning with the index finger (Figs. 12-1 to 12-4). Repeat several times. Encourage your child to do it. Assist the child as needed. When comfortable with the activity, recite the following as you do it:

> Pinch a one, pinch a two, pinch a three and four.
> Pinch your fingers, one by one. Let's do it, once
>   more.
> Pinch a one, pinch a two, pinch a three and four.

Figure 12-1

Figure 12-2

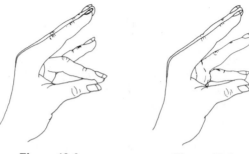

Figure 12-3   **Figure 12-4**

Language Development (1–5 Years Old)

Jabber, Jabber

SUBJECT:	Language development
LEVEL:	1 year old
PURPOSE:	Promote language Expose language patterns to the child
MATERIALS:	None
PROCEDURE:	Talk to the child while driving along the road. Talk about the things you see, the place you are driving to. It's okay if the child doesn't understand you. This helps the child learn language patterns and the importance of language. Sing to the child.

Puppet Pal

SUBJECT:	Language development
LEVEL:	1 year old and up
PURPOSE:	Develop language ability Entertain child

MATERIALS: Puppet(s) of any kind

PROCEDURE: Utilize puppets in the car to keep the child entertained. Talk to the child with the puppets. This will encourage language and demonstrate language patterns.

Guess What I Am

SUBJECT: Language development

LEVEL: 1 1/2 years old and up

PURPOSE: To teach the child to identify something by the sound it makes

MATERIALS: None

PROCEDURE: Tell the child to listen. Make a noise of something specific that you know the child will be able to identify or that you would like to teach him to identify. Some suggestions could be a car, motorcycle, airplane, boat, etc.

Zoo Trip

SUBJECT: Language development

LEVEL: 1 1/2 years old and up

PURPOSE: Develop language skills
Encourage dramatic play

MATERIALS: Pictures of zoo animals (optional)

PROCEDURE: While driving in your car, pretend you are driving through the zoo. Have the child hold the pictures if you choose to use them or simply name any zoo animal. As each animal is selected, act out the noises it makes. Pretend to be the animal selected. After a minute, select another animal and do the same.

NOTE: This is an activity that can be done almost anywhere.

Fire Engine, Fire Engine

SUBJECT: Language development/Safety

LEVEL: 2 years and up

PURPOSE: Develop listening skills and recall
              Awareness of fire safety

MATERIALS: None

PROCEDURE: While you are driving in the car, you may hear sirens
              blow or see a fire truck go by. This would be a great
              time to teach your child this verse, as well as any other
              time. Follow this procedure to help the child learn it:

> *Tell the child:* "Listen first and then repeat what I
> said with me."
> *Say:* "The fire engine goes woo, woo, woo."
> Then have the child repeat it with you.
> *Say:* "The horn goes beep, beep, beep."
> Have the child repeat it with you.
> *Say:* "The fireman says, 'You better hurry up.'"
> Have the child repeat it with you.
> *Say:* "so we can put the fire out!"
> Have the child repeat it.

NOTE: As the child becomes more and more familiar with the
              words, she will sing the song with you, instead of
              repeating it line by line.

Row, Row, Row Your Boat

SUBJECT: Language development

LEVEL: 2 years old and up

PURPOSE: Develop language skills

MATERIALS: None

PROCEDURE: Teach the child the song, "Row, Row, Row Your
              Boat":

Row, row, row your boat, gently down the stream.
Merrily, merrily, merrily, merrily,
Life is but a DREAM.

After teaching the child the words, change the word *dream* to your child's name. Then replace it with other names familiar to the child (i.e., mommy, daddy, grandma, grandpa).

VARIATION: Change the word *dream* to familiar things. Look at the things around you (i.e., trees, clouds, cars, red light).

Things Around You

SUBJECT: Language development

LEVEL: 2 1/2 years old

PURPOSE: Develop ability to identify objects by use

MATERIALS: Common items, i.e., shoes, hairbrush, hat, gloves

PROCEDURE: Keep in mind that the child learns from what surrounds him and what is said to him. The child needs many practical experiences with everyday things along with the language that accompanies these experiences. Practice explaining to the child what he is doing during daily routine activities as you say the following:

"Your shoes go on your feet."
"You brush your hair with a hairbrush."
"You wear a hat on your head."
"You wear gloves on your hands."
"You sit in your seat."

Name That Action

SUBJECT: Language development

LEVEL: 2 1/2 years old

PURPOSE: Develop ability to identify common actions

MATERIALS: None

PROCEDURE: Children need to be exposed to concrete experiences involving actions and names for these actions. Help her to describe her actions throughout your daily routine of activities. It is an important language builder:

> "You are sitting in your car seat."
> "Rachel is clapping to the music."
> "Daddy is driving the car."

Teach the child actions words as she performs them. Name an action for the child to perform. Demonstrate if needed.

Name That Tune

SUBJECT: Language development

LEVEL: 3 1/2 years old

PURPOSE: Develop listening skills

MATERIALS: None

PROCEDURE: Think of songs your child may be familiar with such as "Twinkle, Twinkle, Little Star," "Bah, Bah, Black Sheep," "Rock-a-Bye Baby." Once the child is familiar with the song, hum the song and ask the child to name the song. As a variation, ask the child to sing the song that you name.

Out, In, On . . .

SUBJECT: Language development

LEVEL: 3 1/2 years old and up

PURPOSE: Develop understanding of key words

MATERIALS: None

PROCEDURE: • When near your car, tell the child that both of you are now OUT of the car. Take the keys out of your pocket. Tell the child that you took the keys OUT of your pocket.
• Open the door. Tell the child to get IN the car. Assist the child in buckling his seatbelt. Tell him that you are now putting ON his seatbelt.
• Get in the car. Tell the child, "I am IN the car." Buckle your seatbelt. Tell the child, "I am putting ON my seatbelt."
• Put the keys in the ignition. Tell the child that the key is IN the ignition.
• Continue to stress these key words to the child as you drive.
• Ask the child questions that contain these key words.

NOTE: For more practice with these key words, see the activity "In, Under, On" (pp. 217–218).

Silly Phrases

SUBJECT: Language development

LEVEL: 4 years old

PURPOSE: Develop ability to correct verbal absurdities

MATERIALS: None

PROCEDURE: Tell the child a story with verbal absurdities in it. While driving along, make up any silly phrase: "See the dog flying in the sky. I can see it with my ears. The dog is going to run into the tree. He better watch out before he crashes. Whew! He just missed it. Look! He is walking over to the tree. That dog is talking to the tree. Maybe he is saying 'Sorry for almost crashing into you.' The tree might have cried if the dog flew into him." Encourage the child to correct the absurdities.

This Is What Happened

SUBJECT: Language development

LEVEL: 4 years old

PURPOSE: Develop ability to give an account of daily experiences

MATERIALS: None

PROCEDURE: While driving along in the car, talk with the child about what she has experienced so far that day. Ask the child, "What did you do today that you liked the most?" "Where did you go after breakfast today?" Don't force long responses. Length of responses will vary depending on the child.

VARIATION: After her responses, ask the child if she could put some of them in their order of occurrence.

What Begins with the Letter . . . ?

SUBJECT: Language development

LEVEL: 4 and 5 years old

PURPOSE: Teach letter sounds
Develop language skills

MATERIALS: None

PROCEDURE: Pick a letter for the day. Teach the child the name of the letter and the sound it makes. Look for objects that begin with that letter as you are driving along. Help the child to find things. Allow the child to find things on his own. Give guidance as needed.

NOTE: The activity, "Make Your Own Book" (pp. 75–77), can be used along with this one. This is also a fun activity to do at the park.

I Know My Senses

SUBJECT: Language development

LEVEL: 5 years old

PURPOSE: Develop ability to identify use of senses

MATERIALS: None

PROCEDURE: Teach the child the following (point to each part of your body as you say it):

> I see with my eyes—LOOK
> Look, see the clouds in the sky.
> I hear with my ears—LISTEN
> Listen, hear the engine of the car.
> I smell with my nose—BREATHE
> Breathe in, smell the pretty flowers.
> I taste with my mouth—TASTE
> Eat and taste the delicious ice cream.
> I touch with my hands—FEEL
> Feel the roof of the car.

Little Bo Peep

SUBJECT: Language development

LEVEL: 5 years old

PURPOSE: Develop language skills (rhymes)

MATERIALS: None

PROCEDURE:
- Say the following to the child: "Little Bo PEEP, lost her SHEEP."
- Tell the child that "peep" and "sheep" rhyme. Give your child another example: "Little Bo PEAR, Lost her BEAR." Continue with this, but now you say the first part and have the child find the correct rhyming word. Here are some more examples:

> Little Bo Pow, lost her cow
> Little Bo Word, lost her bird
> Little Bo Pat, lost her cat
> Little Bo Log, lost her dog
> Little Bo Course, lost her horse

Picture Story

SUBJECT:	Language development
LEVEL:	5 years old
PURPOSE:	Develop ability to tell a story by looking at and describing pictures
MATERIALS:	Familiar story books Picture cards
PROCEDURE:	• *Prerequisite:* Begin reading at home. See the activity, "Picture Story"(pp. 94–95). • With very familiar books or picture cards, ask the child to "read the book" to you or tell you what is going on in the pictures while you are driving.

Mathematics (2 1/2–5 Years Old)

Tap Counting

SUBJECT:	Mathematics/Counting
LEVEL:	3 years old and up
PURPOSE:	Count according to taps
MATERIALS:	None
PROCEDURE:	Tap your hand on the dashboard three times and say, "One, two, three. Now let's hear you count with me." Count and tap with the child. Increase the numbers gradually. Tell the child to listen while you tap and count. Then have the child count with you while you tap. *Goals:* 3 years old—up to 3; 4 years old—up to 10; 4 1/2 years old—up to 15; 5 years old—up to 20.
VARIATIONS:	Sing the numbers with the child. Tap on the seat of your car and count.

Shoe Box Count

SUBJECT: Mathematics

LEVEL: 2 1/2 years old and up

PURPOSE: Develop ability to give the number of objects as requested

MATERIALS: 5 small blocks
Shoebox for blocks

PROCEDURE:
- *2 1/2 years old—give one object:* Pull one block out of the box and tell the child that this is one. Give her one block and say this is one. Then tell her to give you one. Put all the blocks in the shoe box. Ask the child to give you one block. Reinforce the one object by showing her one block. Praise the child when she shows or hands you one block.
- *3 years old—give up to three blocks:* Count the blocks in the shoebox. Tell the child that there are five blocks in the box. Have the child say, "Five blocks." Point to each block and count, "One, two, three, four, five." Have the child repeat. Ask the child to give you two blocks. Assist her as needed. Praise her for correct response.
- *4–5 years old—give five objects:* Repeat same as above. Ask for four blocks instead of two. Assist the child as needed. Praise her for correct response.

Rhythm Tapping

SUBJECT: Mathematics/Ordering

LEVEL: 4 years old

PURPOSE: Develop listening skills: ability to hear and repeat a pattern

MATERIALS: None

PROCEDURE: Have the child listen as you tap a rhythm on the dash-
board or seat of the car (for example, tap, tap . . .
pause . . . tap, tap, tap). Tell him to clap or tap the same
pattern that you tapped. Start out simple and progres-
sively make the rhythms a little more complicated.
Work within a range to ensure success for the child.

Traffic Light, Traffic Light

SUBJECT: Mathematics/Classification

LEVEL: 4 years old and up

PURPOSE: Identify colors red and green on a traffic signal: red—
STOP; green—GO

MATERIALS: None

PROCEDURE: When you come to a traffic light on the road, tell the
child its color and what it means. Then say and do the
following: "The light is red, so I need to stop." Stop the
car at the light. When the light turns green, say, "The
light is green, so now I can go." Proceed to drive on.
Continue this with each traffic light you come to. Ask
the child what color it is and what it means.

Personal–Social Skills (4–5 Years Old)

The Street Where You Live

SUBJECT: Personal–social skills

LEVEL: 4 years old

PURPOSE: Correctly give house number and street name of your
residence

MATERIALS: None

PROCEDURE: Tell the child the name of the street she lives on. Have
her repeat the street name. Put the name of the street
to a rap rhythm. Have it go something like this:

> I live on a street that's called
> Laurel Drive, you see . . .
> Yes, Laurel Drive is my street.
> The street on which I live.
> Yes, Laurel Drive.
> I said Laurel Drive.

Then teach the child her house number on that street. Add it to the lyrics:

> Now on that street called Laurel Drive
> My house is number 91.
> My address is 91.
> 91 Laurel Drive.
> So when you ask me where I live
> I'll say, 91 Laurel Drive.

Then ask the child, "Where do you live?" Have child say the complete address.

Happy, Sad, or Mad?

SUBJECT: Personal–social skills

LEVEL: 5 years old

PURPOSE: Develop ability to name and describe emotions

MATERIALS: None

PROCEDURE:
- Teach the child the song "If You're Happy and You Know It":

  > If you're happy and you know it
  > Clap your hands (clap, clap)
  > If you're happy and you know it
  > Clap your hands (clap, clap)
  > If you're happy and you know it
  > Then your face will surely show it (smile)
  > If you're happy and you know it
  > Clap your hands (clap, clap)

If you're mad and you know it
Tap your hand (tap, tap)
If you're mad and you know it
Tap your hand (tap, tap)
If you're mad and you know it
Then your face will surely show it (scowl)
If you're mad and you know it
Tap your hand (tap, tap)

If you're sad and you know it
Cry boo hoo, boo hoo (wipe eyes)
If you're sad and you know it
Cry boo hoo, boo hoo (wipe eyes)
If you're sad and you know it
Then your face will surely show it (frown)
If you're sad and you know it
Cry boo hoo, boo hoo (wipe eyes).
But . . .
If you're happy and you know it
Clap your hands (clap, clap)
If you're happy and you know it
Clap your hands (clap, clap)
If you're happy and you know it
Then your face will surely show it (smile)
If you're happy and you know it
Clap your hands (clap, clap).

- After doing this song, smile at the child. Ask him "How do I feel?" Response should be happy. If he is not responding correctly, give choices, e.g., "Am I happy or sad?"
- Scowl at the child. Ask him "Now, how do I feel?" Answer should be mad or angry. If child does not respond correctly, give choices.
- Look sad, wipe your eyes and say, "boo hoo." Ask the child, "How do I feel?" Child should respond by saying sad. If child is unable to answer correctly, give

choices. Work with the child on emotions until he is able to recognize what they are by name. This will help the child to express his own emotions, e.g., "I feel sad."

Science (5 1/2 Years Old)

The Weather Report

SUBJECT: Science

LEVEL: 5 1/2 years old

PURPOSE: Develop ability to describe weather conditions

MATERIALS: None

PROCEDURE: Describe the weather with the child as much as possible. Look outside and talk about the weather with the child. When discussing the weather with her, ask, "How does it look outside today?" When you leave the car, ask "How does it feel outside today?" Assist the child as needed using descriptive terms like cold, hot, chilly, raining, snowing, windy, cloudy, sunny.

Chapter 13

Activities at the Store

INTRODUCTION

As you enter the store with a child, she may be overloaded with stimuli, such as bright lights, many colors, people, little children and babies, music playing, or a voice over the loudspeaker. You will want to direct the child's energies and excitement into positive actions and maintain appropriate behavior.

In stores with carts, put the child in the seat. Buckle him in if there is a strap. If you're in a store that does not have carts, put the child in his stroller. Be sure he is strapped in. Be sure that an older child, too big for a stroller, holds your hand.

The activities in this chapter are geared to keep the child entertained in order to avoid boredom, restlessness, and other undesirable behaviors, as well as to provide opportunities for development in various areas. Remember, children have short attention spans. Shopping can often be boring for children and cause them to become restless. Utilize these activities to occupy the child's attention while you shop. Include the child in the decision-making process when selecting items. Doing so can make the child feel important and responsible. It's also a great learning process for her. What a great feeling it is for a child to help mommy and daddy "decide," even though you make the final decision. This will help build the child's self-esteem.

ACTIVITIES

Although the following fingerplay activities can be played almost anywhere, they are especially entertaining while waiting on line at the checkout counter.

Fine Motor Skills (3–5 Years Old)

Here's a Bunny

Here's a bunny with ears so funny (hold up index and middle fingers)
And here is a hole in the ground (make a circle with other hand)
With each noise he hears (bring down index and middle fingers)
He pricks up his ears (bring index and middle fingers back up)
And jumps in the hole in the ground (put index and middle fingers into circle made with other hand).

Open, Shut Them

Open, shut them (open and close hands)
Open, shut them
Give a little clap (clap your hands)
Open, shut them
Open, shut them
Put them on your lap (put hands on lap)
Creep them, creep them to your chin (have fingers crawl up to your chin)
But don't let them in.

Wiggle My Fingers

I wiggle my fingers (wiggle fingers)
I wiggle my toes (wiggle toes)
I wiggle my shoulders (wiggle shoulders)

I wiggle my nose (wiggle nose)
Now I have all my wiggles out of me
And I can sit as nice as can be.

Grandma's Glasses

Here are grandma's glasses (make circles around your eyes with
   your fingers)
Here is grandma's hat (make a hat with your hands on your head)
This is the way she folds her hands and puts them on her lap
(fold hands together and put them on your lap).
(In a deep voice) Here are grandpa's glasses
Here is grandpa's hat
This is the way he folds his arms and puts them on his lap
(fold arms and put them on your lap).

Thumbkin

SUBJECT: Fine motor skills

LEVEL: 3 years old

PURPOSE: Develop ability to wiggle thumb and fingers individ-
             ually while other fingers are closed into a fist

MATERIALS: None

PROCEDURE: Sing the following song with the child to the tune of
             "Are You Sleeping":

             (Begin with both hands behind your back)
             Where is thumbkin? (wiggle thumb, right hand)
             Where is thumbkin?
             Here I am! (wiggle thumb, left hand)
             Here I am!
             How are you today, sir? (wiggle thumb, right
             hand)
             Very well, I thank you (wiggle thumb, left hand)
             Run away (move right hand behind your back)
             Run away (move left hand behind your back).

Repeat the verse by substituting "pointer," "tall man," "ring man," and "pinky" to represent the other fingers.

Pinch A One . . .

SUBJECT:	Fine motor skills
LEVEL:	4 and 5 years old
PURPOSE:	Develop ability to grasp with finger and thumb
	Develop coordination in hand, muscle control
MATERIALS:	None
PROCEDURE:	• Demonstrate spreading fingers wide with your palm facing the child. While the child is watching, touch your thumb with the tip of each finger beginning with the index finger. Repeat several times. Encourage your child to do it. Assist the child as needed.
	• When comfortable with the activity, recite the following as you do it:

Pinch a one, pinch a two, pinch a three and four
Pinch your fingers, one by one. Let's do it, once more.
Pinch a one, pinch a two, pinch a three and four.

NOTE:	See Figs. 12-1 through 12-4 (pp. 189–190), for visual examples.

Gross Motor Skills (1 1/2–5 Years Old)

"I Help you Push"

SUBJECT:	Gross motor skills
LEVEL:	1 1/2 years and up
PURPOSE:	Develop large muscle ability
	Present opportunity for child to be a "helper"
	Prevent child from becoming restless

MATERIALS: Shopping cart

PROCEDURE: Place child directly in between the cart and yourself (Fig. 13-1). Find a comfortable place for the child to hold onto the cart and allow her to help you push the cart throughout the store. When she gets tired, put her in cart seat to rest.

Language Development (1–5 Years Old)

Jabber, Jabber

SUBJECT: Language development

LEVEL: 1 year old

Figure 13-1

PURPOSE: Promote language
              Present language patterns

MATERIALS: None

PROCEDURE: Talk to the child while shopping in the store. It's okay
              if the child doesn't understand you. This helps the
              child learn language patterns and the importance of
              language. Sing songs to the child.

Objects in the Store

SUBJECT: Language development

LEVEL: 1 1/2 years old

PURPOSE: Develop vocabulary

MATERIALS: Any objects around you

PROCEDURE: Point out objects to the child. Tell the child what the
              object is and encourage him to repeat it. Praise him
              immediately after he says the word(s). Take advantage
              of everything around you. Talk to the child. Talk about
              the things you do and see as you go through the store.

Five Little Monkeys

SUBJECT: Language development

LEVEL: 1 1/2 years old and up

PURPOSE: Promote language development

MATERIALS: None

PROCEDURE: Sing the following song to the child, encouraging her
              to sing with you as she learns the words and actions:

> (*Hold up five fingers*) Five little monkeys,
> (*swing same hand back and forth*) swinging in a tree,
> Teasing Mr. Alligator (*shake finger back and forth*),
> "Can't catch me" (*put thumbs to each side of your head
> and wiggle your fingers*—see Fig. 13-2)

Figure 13-2

"Nanoo, Nanoo, Nanoo, can't catch me."
(*Whisper words, put hands together and wiggle them back and forth*—Fig. 13-3)
Along came Mr. Alligator, quiet as can be . . .
(*Speak aloud, open hands keeping heel of palms touching*—see Fig. 13-4—*and snap your hands together*)
SNAP!
(*Continue with actions as stated above*)
Four little monkeys swinging in a tree, teasing Mr. Alligator, "Can't catch me. Nanoo, Nanoo, Nanoo. Can't catch me." Along came Mr. Alligator, quiet as can be . . . SNAP!

Continue until you get to "No little monkeys."

NOTE: This activity can be done almost anywhere.

Figure 13-3

Figure 13-4

Guess What I Am

SUBJECT: Language development

LEVEL: 1 1/2 years old and up

PURPOSE: Teach the child to identify something by the sound it makes

MATERIALS: None

PROCEDURE: Tell the child to listen. Make a noise of something specific that you know the child will be able to identify or that you would like to teach him to identify. Some ideas could be emotions (laughing, crying, moaning, etc.), animals (lions, tigers, bears, dogs, cats, etc.).

Pass! Pass!

SUBJECT: Language development

LEVEL: 1 1/2 years old and up

PURPOSE: Develop language skills
Practice rhythm
Develop eye–hand coordination

MATERIALS: None

PROCEDURE: Recite the following verse in a singsong fashion while going through the store:

(French)
Pass! Pass! Passera!
La derniere, la derniere.
Pass! Pass! Passera!
La derniere, RESTERA!

If the child is sitting in a cart facing you, clap your hands to the child's hands (Fig. 13-5) while singing this

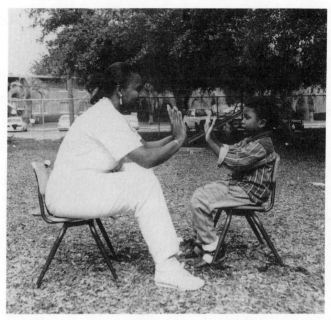

Figure 13-5

verse. If the child is in a stroller or walking along side of you, clap your own hands and encourage the child to do the same (Fig. 13-6). When you come to the word "RESTERA," tickle the child at the waist or give her a hug (in an "I got you" fashion).

NOTE: This is a fun activity to do almost anywhere.

Identify Object by Use

SUBJECT: Language development

LEVEL: 2 1/2 years old

PURPOSE: Develop ability to identify objects by use

Figure 13-6

MATERIALS: Common objects, i.e., shoes, shopping cart

PROCEDURE: Keep in mind that the child learns from what is surrounding him and what is said to him. The child needs many concrete experiences with everyday things and the language that accompanies these experiences. Practice explaining to the child what he is doing during daily routine activities and encourage the child to say the following:

> "Your shoes go on your feet."
> "You sit in the cart."
> "You walk in the store."
> "Food goes in the shopping cart."

Name That Action

SUBJECT: Language development

LEVEL: 2 1/2 years old

PURPOSE: Develop ability to identify common actions

MATERIALS: None

PROCEDURE: Children need to be exposed to concrete experiences
doing things and naming these actions. Help the child
to describe her actions throughout your daily routine
of activities. It is an important language builder.

> "You are sitting in the cart."
> "Kelsey is helping mommy push the cart."
> "Mommy is paying for the food."

Say the action words as she performs them. Name an
action for the child to perform. Demonstrate if needed.

Which One Would You Like?

SUBJECT: Language development

LEVEL: 3 years old and up

PURPOSE: Name preferred object when given a choice
Develop decision-making process

MATERIALS: Items in the store

PROCEDURE: When at the store, encourage the child to be your
helper. Give the child experience in making choices. If
you're buying juice, allow the child to select from two
choices of items that you would agree to buy. Continue
to do this throughout the store.

Pass It On

SUBJECT: Language development

LEVEL: 3 1/2 years old

PURPOSE: Develop ability to listen to a message and tell it to someone else

MATERIALS: None

PROCEDURE: When ordering something over the counter or communicating with the cashier, tell the child what you need to say and have him ask for it (Fig. 13-7). Praise the child for his success (or attempt). If he is not comfortable in talking with the individual, it's okay. Try again next time.

In, Under, On

SUBJECT: Language development

LEVEL: 4 years old and up

Figure 13-7

PURPOSE: Follow verbal commands using key words: in, in front of, beside, behind, under, on

MATERIALS: None

PROCEDURE: While you are in the store, give the child verbal commands for key words. Here are some examples:

> Put the food IN the cart.
> See the little girl standing IN FRONT OF us.
> Please stand BESIDE me.
> Say "hi" to the lady BEHIND us.
> Mommy put the diapers UNDER the cart.
> The bread is ON the rack.

NOTE: For more practice with these key words, see the activity, "Out, In, On" (pp. 194–195).

This Is What Happened

SUBJECT: Language development

LEVEL: 4 years old

PURPOSE: Develop ability to give account of recent experiences in order of occurrence

MATERIALS: None

PROCEDURE: While you are in the store with the child, ask her some questions about what she did prior to going to the store. Ask specific questions to assist her in remembering what she experienced. Questions you could ask are:

> "What did you eat for breakfast?"
> "What did you do before we left for the store?"
> "Where did you sit in the car?"
> "Who did we see on our way into the store?"
> "What did the lady say to you when we came in the store?"

I Know My Senses

SUBJECT:	Language development
LEVEL:	5 years old
PURPOSE:	Develop ability to identify with the senses
MATERIALS:	None
PROCEDURE:	When you take the child to the grocery store, you will find many things to reinforce his ability to identify events with his senses. Here are some ideas:

- "Look at the people. See the little girl."
- "Listen, I hear a baby crying."
- At the deli, they sometimes have a basket or tray of things to nibble. Eat the cracker. It tastes good.
- At the bakery, they often give out free cookies for children. Have the child smell it. Allow your child to eat the cookie. It tastes good.
- In the freezer section, items are cold. Allow the child to feel the cold box of vegetables, the frozen can of apple juice, the cold bag of french fries, etc.

Mathematics (2–5 Years Old)

Repeat This

SUBJECT:	Mathematics/Ordering
LEVEL:	2 years old and up
PURPOSE:	Develop ability to repeat patterns in the correct order
MATERIALS:	None
PROCEDURE:	Start this activity by setting a rhythm. Tell the child to listen and then repeat what you do. For example, first clap a two-beat rhythm:

(you) clap, clap
(child) clap, clap
(you) clap, clap
(child) clap, clap, etc.

Tell the child that you are going to say something and that she has to repeat it:

Say, "Listen: 'dog, cat.' Now you say it.
Here's another one: '2, 1.'" Point to the child to signal to say "2, 1." Continue on with other sets of patterns. Increase them as child progresses successfully.

Goals: 2 years old—repeat two-pattern sequence; 3 years old—repeat three-pattern sequence; 4 1/2 years old—repeat four-pattern sequence.

A Color Walk

SUBJECT:	Mathematics/Classification
LEVEL:	2 1/2 years old
PURPOSE:	Develop ability to name one color when shown objects of different colors
MATERIALS:	Any objects in the store
PROCEDURE:	"Let's begin with the color green. Today we're going to take a green walk while we're shopping." Have the child look for green objects throughout the store. Point out a green object to the child before you have him begin. Ask him if the objects you are buying are green or not. Pick a different color each time you shop.

Big and Little

SUBJECT:	Mathematics
LEVEL:	3 years old

PURPOSE: Develop ability to recognize big and little objects

MATERIALS: Big and little objects

PROCEDURE: Point out objects that are big and little. For every big object, show the child a little object. Show the child a big box of laundry detergent, then a small box of laundry detergent. Show an orange and a cantaloupe. Ask her to point to the big object. Continue this with other objects in the store. Assist the child as needed.

Counting Objects One by One

SUBJECT: Mathematics/Counting

LEVEL: 3 1/2 years old and up

PURPOSE: Develop ability to count objects

MATERIALS: Anything

PROCEDURE: Count objects aloud for the child to hear you. Have the child count with you. Encourage the child to point to each object as you both count items such as plums, apples, grapes, cans of vegetables, fresh rolls, etc.
Goals: 3 1/2 years old—three objects; 4 1/2 years old—four objects; 5 years old—ten objects; 5 1/2 years old—13 objects.

Things That Are Long

SUBJECT: Mathematics

LEVEL: 3 1/2 years old

PURPOSE: Develop concept of long objects

MATERIALS: Long objects

PROCEDURE: • Point out long objects to the child while going through the store such as a loaf of French bread; a night gown; hair ribbon.
            • Show the child some short objects for comparison. Have the child find objects that are long.

All Gone

SUBJECT:	Mathematics
LEVEL:	3 1/2 years old
PURPOSE:	Teach concept of empty
MATERIALS:	Shopping cart
	Cups and beverage
	Container and salad

PROCEDURE:

- When you arrive at the store, get a shopping cart in which to put your items. Tell the child that the cart is empty as you show it to him. As you put items in the cart tell him, "The cart is not empty anymore because we put things in it." After you finish shopping and load your bags in the car, tell the child that the cart is now empty again.
- Many deli's in the store have a soda fountain available for public use. Take the child to it. Take a cup and show the child that the cup is empty. Put a beverage in the cup. Tell the child, "I filled the empty cup with Sprite. Now the cup is full." Take another cup and tell the child that this cup is empty. Ask the child which of the two cups is empty.
- The salad from the deli department provides another demonstration. Show the child the empty container, telling him it is empty. Put the salad in the container. Show it to the child, telling him it is now full. Take another container and tell him it is empty. Ask the child which container is empty.

Is It A . . . ?

SUBJECT:	Mathematics/Classification
LEVEL:	3 1/2 years old and up
PURPOSE:	Classify objects by pointing

MATERIALS: Things around you at the store

PROCEDURE: While in the grocery store, teach the child how to classify groups of items. Here are some classifications for items you will find in the grocery store:

Breads	Lunchmeat	Sauces
Meats	Fruit	Fish
Snacks	Vegetables	Animal food
Pasta	Beverages	Cereal
Frozen foods		

Classifications you will find in other stores are:

Hardware	Electronics
Men's clothing	Housewares
Infant/Toddler	Boy's clothing
Shoes	Women's clothing
Health and beauty aids	Car accessories

Now point to an item in the store and give them two classifications from which to choose. For example, ask if the roll is a bread or a meat. Assist the child as needed.

Hard and Soft

SUBJECT: Mathematics/Classification

LEVEL: 4 1/2 years old

PURPOSE: Differentiate between hard and soft

MATERIALS: Pairs of hard and soft textures such as apple, peach; baseball, sponge ball; mop handle, sponge; cutting board, paper towel.

PROCEDURE: Present pairs of hard–soft objects to the child. Name the hard and soft objects and have the child touch each. After a few pairs, allow the child to touch the objects

and tell you if it is hard or soft. Assist the child as
needed.

Money, Money

SUBJECT: Mathematics/Classification

LEVEL: 4 1/2 years old and up

PURPOSE: Develop ability to identify coins

MATERIALS: Quarter, dime, nickel, penny

PURPOSE: • When it comes time to pay for items you are buying
             in the store, allow the child to be included. If you are
             paying with some coins, hand them to the child,
             naming each coin as you place it in her hand. Have
             the child hand the coins to the cashier.
             • If you receive coins back with your change, present
             an opportunity to name the coins. See how many
             coins the child can name.

There's the Circle (Triangle, Square, Rectangle)

SUBJECT: Mathematics/Geometry

LEVEL: 4 1/2 to 5 years old

PURPOSE: Develop ability to point to the shape specified

MATERIALS: Objects that are shaped like a circle, triangle, square,
             and rectangle

PROCEDURE: • While you are in the store, look around you to see
             what shapes you can find. Only teach the child one
             shape at a time. Begin with the circle. Point out
             objects in the store that are shaped like a circle such
             as pie plates, hula hoops, oranges, and cupcakes. Tell
             the child that each of these things are shaped like a
             circle. Encourage the child to find things that are
             shaped like a circle.
             • Do the same thing with the triangle, square, and
             rectangle.

- Many stores have pictures hanging from the ceiling. See what shapes they are. Look at pictures hanging on the wall. You may find shapes in the pictures to show the child.

Color It Blue, Red . . .

SUBJECT:	Mathematics/Classification
LEVEL:	5 years old
PURPOSE:	Develop ability to identify the colors blue, red, yellow, and green
MATERIALS:	Objects throughout the store that are blue, red, yellow, and green
PROCEDURE:	While shopping in the store have the child identify objects of the colors blue, red, yellow, or green. Point out objects to the child that contain these colors. Some items you may find in the grocery store are blue Windex (window cleaner), red apples, yellow bananas, green cucumbers.

First and Last

SUBJECT:	Mathematics/Classification
LEVEL:	5 years old
PURPOSE:	Ability to recognize first and last
MATERIALS:	None
PROCEDURE:	When you and the child are walking through the store where you need to move single file, allow the child to go first, telling him he is FIRST. While waiting in a line for something or when it is time to check out with the cashier, tell the child that you are LAST in line. Point out to the child the person who is FIRST in line. When you get up to the front, tell the child you are now FIRST in line.

Which One Is Bigger?

SUBJECT: Mathematics/Classification

LEVEL: 5 1/2 years old

PURPOSE: Develop understanding of bigger

MATERIALS: Pairs of objects: little–big

PROCEDURE: Show the child big and little objects of the same type, i.e., cucumbers, bananas, apples, pencils, paper, books, cereal boxes. Talk about the objects with the child. Show the child the bigger of the objects. Ask the child which is bigger. Compare objects of different kinds such as an apple and a grapefruit; a loaf of bread and a box of cereal. Ask the child which is bigger.

Chapter 14

Activities Anywhere

INTRODUCTION

Almost *anywhere* you go, you see things that can be taught to your child. Remember, when your child was born, all he had experienced was life in the womb. The activities we expose our child to by using all the senses—seeing, hearing, smelling, feeling, and tasting—enable our child to learn as he grows and develops. As the child watches the leaves turning colors during autumn, he is visually experiencing what happens in nature during this season. When parents talk to their children, they are learning language patterns and vocabulary. Finger plays develop language, small muscle ability, and eye–hand coordination. Since the activities in this chapter can be carried out in almost any type of setting (for example, at grandma's house, in a fast-food restaurant, on the way to the store, etc.), some of the more suitable activities from prior chapters are repeated or modified below. There are also many new activities for this chapter.

Remember to supervise the child closely as needed. Work with the child at her pace. Try not to aggravate or frustrate the child. Keep learning fun. Give the child quality time. Interact with her as much as possible. You are a role model for the child *anywhere* you go with her.

ACTIVITIES

Fine Motor Skills (3–5 Years Old)

Pennies in the Bank

SUBJECT:	Fine motor skills
LEVEL:	3 years old
PURPOSE:	Develop ability to put smaller objects into larger objects Develop ability to pick up small objects Practice counting
MATERIALS:	Pennies Piggybank
PROCEDURE:	Place pennies and bank in front of the child. Demonstrate picking up a penny and putting it inside the bank through the slot. Have the child try it. Give assistance as needed. Count the pennies as you put them in the bank.

Thumbkin

SUBJECT:	Fine motor skills
LEVEL:	3 years old
PURPOSE:	Develop ability to wiggle thumb and fingers individually while other fingers are closed into a fist
MATERIALS:	None
PROCEDURE:	Sing the following song with the child to the tune of "Are you Sleeping":

> (Begin with both hands behind your back)
> Where is thumbkin? (wiggle thumb, right hand)
> Where is thumbkin?
> Here I am! (wiggle thumb, left hand)
> Here I am!
> How are you today, sir? (wiggle thumb, right hand)

Very well, I thank you (wiggle thumb, left hand)
Run away (move right hand behind your back)
Run away (move left hand behind your back)

Repeat the verse by substituting "pointer," "tall man," "ring man," and "pinky" to represent the other fingers.

Pinch a One . . .

SUBJECT:	Fine motor skills
LEVEL:	4 and 5 years old
PURPOSE:	Develop ability to grasp with finger and thumb
	Develop coordination in hand, muscle control
MATERIALS:	None
PROCEDURE:	Demonstrate spreading fingers wide with your palm facing the child. While the child is watching, touch your thumb with the tip of each finger beginning with the index finger. Repeat several times. Encourage your child to do it. Assist the child as needed. When comfortable with the activity, recite the following as you do it:

Pinch a one, pinch a two, pinch a three and four
Pinch your fingers, one by one. Let's do it, once
more.
Pinch a one, pinch a two, pinch a three and four.

NOTE:	See Figs. 12-1 through 12-4 (pp. 189–190) for visual examples.

Gross Motor Skills (3–5 Years Old)

A Duck on One Foot

SUBJECT:	Gross motor skills
LEVEL:	3 years old

PURPOSE: Develop ability to stand on one foot without losing
            balance

MATERIALS: None

PROCEDURE: Act like ducks. Walk with a waddle and say "quack,
            quack." Stand in place and lift one foot for one second.
            Demonstrate this to the child; then have her do it with
            you.

NOTE: As the child gets older, gradually increase requirements
            for standing on one foot.
            Goals: 4 years old—5 seconds; 5 years old—with hands
            across chest; stand on each foot alternately.

Attention

SUBJECT: Gross motor skills/ Personal–social skills

LEVEL: 3 years old and up

PURPOSE: Develop ability of keeping balance
            Strengthen self-control

MATERIALS: None

PROCEDURE: Demonstrate "attention" to the child by standing still
            with your feet together and arms at your side. Have the
            child do it. Tell the child that when you say "Atten-
            tion," he is to stand that way. Have him hold the
            position for 5 seconds or more to increase balance
            ability. Count out loud with the child—1, 2, etc.

VARIATION: Whenever you find the child is getting "unruly" and
            demonstrating inappropriate behavior, tell him, "At-
            tention." Count to ten (gives you time to collect your-
            self). When the child demonstrates ability of self-con-
            trol, resume activity.

Ballerina Child

SUBJECT: Gross motor skills

LEVEL: 3 years old and up

PURPOSE: Develop ability to stand and walk on tiptoes

MATERIALS: None

PROCEDURE: Tell the child, "Let's pretend that we are ballerinas." First practice standing on your tiptoes. Have the child try it. Once the child is comfortable with that, demonstrate how to walk on your tiptoes for approximately 10 feet. Have the child walk on her tiptoes. Encourage her to keep her arms extended for balance. When the child reaches about the age of 5, have her stand on her toes with her hands on her hips.

Language Development

Jabber, Jabber

SUBJECT: Language development

LEVEL: 1 year old

PURPOSE: Promote language
Expose language patterns to the child

MATERIALS: None

PROCEDURE:
- Talk to the child during normal activities of the day (changing diaper, dressing, feeding, bathing, playing, driving, shopping). It's okay if the child doesn't understand you. This helps the child learn language patterns and the importance of language.
- Sing to the child. Read simple picture books to the child on a daily basis. A routine story time is very beneficial for the child. He will adapt easily to the new schedule.

Ticklebug

SUBJECT: Language development

LEVEL: 1 year old and up

PURPOSE: Develop listening skills
             Develop imagination

MATERIALS: None

PROCEDURE: Tell the child something like this: "I've got something
             in my pocket. Oh, it's tickling me. Let me see if I can
             get it out of my pocket." Put your hand in your pock-
             et. Bring your hand out of your pocket with a closed
             fist like you are holding something in your hand. Peek
             into your closed hand without opening your fist.
             "There's a ticklebug in my hand. Would you like to
             see it?" If the child responds "yes," open your hand
             and quickly and gently tickle the child. "The ticklebug
             is tickling you. Oh no, let me get him back in my
             hand." Stop tickling the child and close your hand.
             "I've got him back in my hand." If the child wants to
             see the ticklebug again, continue the same way. When
             you open your hand, quickly and gently tickle the
             child. Allow the child to hold the ticklebug and tickle
             you sometimes, too.

Five Little Monkeys

SUBJECT: Language development

LEVEL: 1 1/2 years old and up

PURPOSE: Promote language development

MATERIALS: None

PROCEDURE: Sing the following song to the child, encouraging him
             to sing with you as he learns the words and actions:

> (*Hold up five fingers*) Five little monkeys
> (*swing same hand back and forth*) swinging in a tree,
> Teasing Mr. Alligator (*shake finger back and forth*)
> "Can't catch me." (*put thumbs to each side of your head
> and wiggle your fingers*)
> "Nanoo, Nanoo, Nanoo, can't catch me."

(*Whisper words, put hands together and wiggle them back and forth*) Along came Mr. Alligator, quiet as can be . . .
(*Speak aloud, open hands keeping heel of palms touching, and snap your hands together*)
SNAP!
(*Continue with actions as stated above*)
Four little monkeys swinging in a tree, teasing Mr. Alligator, "Can't catch me. Nanoo, Nanoo, Nanoo. Can't catch me." Along came Mr. Alligator, quiet as can be, SNAP!
(*Continue until you get to "No little monkeys."*)

Good Manners

SUBJECT: Language development

LEVEL: 1 1/2 years and up

PURPOSE: Develop personal–social skills
Develop proper vocabulary for interacting with others

MATERIALS: None

PROCEDURE:
- Start exposing the child to good manners while she is young. Demonstrate interacting with others by using the words please, thank-you, excuse me, etc. Be a positive role model.
- As the child grows up, she will speak in the manner to which she has been exposed. Encourage the child to say "please" when asking for something. Do not respond until she says it. Be sure to prompt the child to say "please" before expecting it. When given something, have the child say "thank-you."
- By the age of 4, the child may begin to understand the proper context of when to say each of these words. Continue to prompt the child until you recognize that she understands when it is the appropriate time to use these words.

Guess What I Am

SUBJECT: Language development

LEVEL: 1 1/2 years old and up

PURPOSE: Teach the child to identify something by the sound it makes

MATERIALS: None

PROCEDURE: Tell the child to listen. Make a noise of something specific that you know the child will be able to identify or that you would like to teach him to identify. Some suggestions are animals, vehicles, and people.

Head, Shoulders, Knees, and Toes

SUBJECT: Language development

LEVEL: 1 1/2 years old and up

PURPOSE: Teach body parts
             Encourage child to verbalize each body part

MATERIALS: None

PROCEDURE: Teach the child the following body parts: head, shoulders, knees, toes, eyes, ears, nose, mouth. Sing the following to the child, touching each body part as you sing it:

> Head, shoulders, knees and toes, knees and toes.
> Head, shoulders, knees and toes and
> eyes and ears and mouth and nose.
> Head, shoulders, knees and toes.

VARIATION: As the child gets older try this with her: *first verse:* replace the word "head" by humming; *second verse:* replace the words "head" and "shoulders" by humming; *third verse:* replace the words "head," "shoulders," and "knees" by humming; *fourth verse:* replace the phrase "head, shoulders, knees and toes" by humming.

Name That Object

SUBJECT:	Language development
LEVEL:	1 1/2 years old and up
PURPOSE:	Develop vocabulary
MATERIALS:	Any objects around you
PROCEDURE:	Point out objects to the child. Tell the child what it is and encourage him to repeat it. Praise him for saying the word immediately after he says it. Take advantage of everything around you throughout the day. Talk to the child. Describe what he is doing. As you play, talk together about the things you do and see.

Pass! Pass!

SUBJECT:	Language development
LEVEL:	1 1/2 years old and up
PURPOSE:	Develop language skills Practice rhythm Develop eye–hand coordination
MATERIALS:	None
PROCEDURE:	Recite the following verse in a singsong fashion:

> (French)
> Pass! Pass! Passera!
> La derniere, la derniere.
> Pass! Pass! Passera!
> La derniere, RESTERA!

(See pp. 213–214 for the rest of the procedures.)

Simon Says

SUBJECT:	Language development
LEVEL:	1 1/2 years old and up

PURPOSE: Follow one-step directions

MATERIALS: Any objects around you practical for a small child to safely handle

PROCEDURE: Stoop down to eye level with the child. Tell her to pick up the block. If the child does not pick it up, assist her to do so. Be sure to praise her for picking up the block. Continue with other objects around you. Be sure to be specific in your directions and praise her for what she does. Try to phrase all directions in a positive manner.

Zoo Trip

SUBJECT: Language development

LEVEL: 1 1/2 years old and up

PURPOSE: Develop language skills
                Encourage dramatic play

MATERIALS: Pictures of zoo animals (optional)

PROCEDURE: While anywhere, pretend you are driving through the zoo. Have the child hold the pictures that you choose to use or simply name any zoo animal. As each animal is selected, act out the noises it makes. Pretend to be the animal selected. After a minute, select another animal and do the same.

Row, Row, Row Your Boat

SUBJECT: Language development

LEVEL: 2 years old and up

PURPOSE: Develop language skills

MATERIALS: None

PROCEDURE: Teach the child the song, "Row, Row, Row Your Boat":

                Row, row, row your boat, gently down the stream.
                Merrily, merrily, merrily, merrily,
                Life is but a DREAM.

After teaching the child the words, change the word *dream* to your child's name. Then replace it with other names familiar to the child (i.e., mommy, daddy, grandma, grandpa, names of siblings, etc.)

VARIATION: Change the word *dream* to familiar things. Look at the things around you (i.e., trees, clouds, apple)

Talking in Sentences

SUBJECT: Language development

LEVEL: 2 years old and up

PURPOSE: Develop ability to speak in short, complete sentences and continue to expand the number of words in the sentence

MATERIALS: None

PROCEDURE: When you interact with the child, speak to him in full sentences as much as possible. "Carl needs to sit down." "Sam is coloring." When the child speaks to you and says, for example, "Book" while handing it to you, say to the child, "Read the book, please." Encourage the child to repeat it. When the child reaches up to you making noises to pick him up, wait and then say to your child, "Pick me up please." Repeat it until the child appropriately responds to the sentence you said. Encourage the child to vocalize by speaking in sentences. Converse with the child in full sentences. This will encourage him to speak in full sentences.

Identify Object by Use

SUBJECT: Language development

LEVEL: 2 1/2 years old

PURPOSE: Develop ability to identify objects by use

MATERIALS: Common objects, e.g., shoes, spoon, toothbrush

PROCEDURE: Keep in mind that the child learns from what is surrounding her and what is said to her. The child needs
many concrete experiences with everyday things and
the language that accompanies these experiences. Practice explaining to the child what she is doing during
daily routine activities and encourage the child to do
this also.

"Your shoes go on your feet."
"You eat with your spoon."
"You brush your teeth with your toothbrush."
"A brush is used on your hair."

VARIATION: After many experiences with everyday objects, show
the child pictures in magazines and newspapers and ask
the child to point to the one that we wear on our head
(hat), and so on.

Name That Action

SUBJECT: Language development

LEVEL: 2 1/2 years old

PURPOSE: Develop ability to identify common actions

MATERIALS: None

PROCEDURE: • Children need to be exposed to concrete experiences
doing things and naming these actions. Help the
child to describe his actions throughout your daily
routine of activities. It is an important language
builder.

"You are eating your carrots."
"Shannon is riding her bicycle."
"Daddy is mowing the grass."

Teach the child action words as he performs them.
Name an action for the child to perform. Demonstrate if needed.

- Show the child pictures of a person doing an activity. Ask the child what that person is doing. Assist the child as needed. Have the child do the action he sees in the picture. Demonstrate it for him if he's not sure what to do.

Flannel Board Picture

SUBJECT: Language development/Spatial terms

LEVEL: 3 and 4 years old

PURPOSE: Reinforce the words: in, on, over, under, on top, above, below

MATERIALS:
- Flannel board set up to represent a bridge across a river. (If you do not have a flannel board, glue a piece of felt onto the same size poster board.)
- Felt pieces: cloud, fish, car, boat, airplane, house, flower, etc. (If felt shapes are not available, pictures backed with small pieces of sandpaper adhere nicely.) Have the child discuss the scene. Then allow the child to add a flannel piece in an appropriate place—the cloud above the bridge, the fish under the water, the boat on the water but below the bridge, the car on the bridge, the flower on the land, the plane above the cloud.

Guess What I'm Doing

SUBJECT: Language development

LEVEL: 4 years old

PURPOSE: Define words by doing an action
Tell what is happening by observing an action

MATERIALS: None

PROCEDURE: Act out something and have the child guess what it is, e.g., a frog, brushing your teeth. When the child guesses correctly, let her do the acting and you do the guessing.

This Is What Happened

SUBJECT: Language development

LEVEL: 4 years old

PURPOSE: Develop ability to give account of recent experiences

MATERIALS: None

PROCEDURE: After an event has taken place for the child, talk with him about what he did. Ask the child questions such as:

> "What did you do today?"
> "Who did you see?"
> "What happened?"
> "Did you like it?"
> "Would you like to do it again sometime?"
> "What was the best part of it?"

I Know My Senses

SUBJECT: Language development

LEVEL: 5 years old

PURPOSE: Develop ability to identify use of senses

MATERIALS: None

PROCEDURE: Teach the child the following (point to each part of your body as you say it):

> I see with my eyes—LOOK
>   Look, see the clouds in the sky.
> I hear with my ears—LISTEN
>   Listen, hear the children playing.
> I smell with my nose—BREATHE
>   Breathe in, smell the cookies in the oven.

I taste with my mouth—EAT
Taste the delicious hot dog.
I touch with my hands—FEEL
Feel the soft teddy bear.

Little Bo Peep

SUBJECT: Language development

LEVEL: 5 years old

PURPOSE: Develop language skills—rhymes

MATERIALS: None

PROCEDURE: Say the following to the child: "Little Bo PEEP, lost her SHEEP." Tell the child that peep and sheep rhyme. Give your child another example: "Little Bo PEAR, lost her BEAR." Continue with this, but now you say the first part and have the child do the second part, finding the correct rhyming word. Here are some more examples:

> Little Bo Now, lost her cow
> Little Bo Herd, lost her bird
> Little Bo Hat, lost her bat
> Little Bo Log, lost her dog
> Little Bo Toss, lost her horse

Things Are Made of This

SUBJECT: Language development

LEVEL: 5 years old

PURPOSE: Develop ability to tell what common things are made of

MATERIALS: Take the child to a construction site where new houses are being built

PROCEDURE: Take the child around to different houses in various stages of construction. Talk to the child about the things used to build the house. Show the child all around house.

VARIATIONS: (1) Make paste out of flour and water. Discuss with your child what paste is made of. (2) Take the child to different plants where glass is made, money is printed, etc. Find places in your area where you can go to watch how things are made such as a bakery, picture frame shop, etc. (3) Make the various recipes given in the beginning of Chapter 10 (p. 60).

Mathematics (3–5 Years Old)

Picture Cards

SUBJECT: Mathematics/Sorting

LEVEL: 3 years old

PURPOSE: Help children recognize differences and likenesses

MATERIALS: Set of picture cards with approximately half showing two objects that are identical and the rest showing two objects that differ in some way (Fig. 14-1).

PROCEDURE: Ask your child to put the cards into two piles, the "alike" pile and the "different" pile. For self-checking, the backs of the cards can be colored.

Sorting Blocks

SUBJECT: Mathematics/Sorting

LEVEL: 3 years old

PURPOSE: Give experience in directed sorting
             Teaching colors or shapes

MATERIALS: Attribute blocks
             Three plastic bags

Figure 14-1

PROCEDURE: Say, "Blocks of each color have their own plastic bag. This block is red and it goes in this bag. Find all of the blocks that are the same color and put them in here." Repeat for blue and yellow.

VARIATION: Have the child sort by shape.

Listen and Do

SUBJECT: Mathematics/Counting

LEVEL: 4 years old

PURPOSE: Develop concept of ordinals
            Improve listening skills

MATERIALS: None

PROCEDURE: Begin the game by explaining that you will give three
directions while the child listens. When you say "Go,"
the child must follow the directions in the order given.
"First, touch your head. Second, clap your hands.
Third, touch the floor." As listening skills improve,
more directions may be included.

Listen!

SUBJECT: Mathematics/Ordering

LEVEL: 4 years old

PURPOSE: Develop listening skills
Ability to hear a pattern

MATERIALS: None

PROCEDURE: Have the child listen as you tap a pattern on any suitable surface such as a desk, table, etc. Tell her to tap the
same thing you tapped. Start out simple and progres-
sively make the patterns a little more complicated.
Work within a range to ensure success for the child.

Guess What I Am

SUBJECT: Mathematics/Classification

LEVEL: 4 and 5 years old

PURPOSE: Teach the child to identify an object by the sound it
makes

MATERIALS: Picture cards of things that make identifiable sounds
such as: a dog, a train, a cow, a baby, a fly

PROCEDURE: Have the child begin by choosing a card and holding it
so you cannot see it. He then makes the appropriate
sound and you try and guess the object. When you get
it right, it is your turn to make the noise and the child's
turn to guess what the object is.

What Do I Hear?

SUBJECT: Mathematics/Classification

LEVEL: 5 years old

PURPOSE: Develop listening skills
Reading readiness

MATERIALS: None

PROCEDURE: Allow the child to rest her head on the table and close her eyes. Recite three words, two of which sound alike in some way. Have the child identify the one which doesn't belong:

Big, dark, boy (initial consonants)
train, try, two (initial blends)
doll, chairs, kittens (plurals)
bent, hot, sleep (final consonants)
raining, swing, table (endings)

VARIATIONS: Rhythms—allow the child to listen to two lullabies, and one marching song.

One Is Different

SUBJECT: Mathematics/Classification

LEVEL: 5 years old

PURPOSE: Help the child notice likenesses and differences

MATERIALS: Eight mounted (glue or tape to index card and cover with contact paper for protection) magazine pictures: a cat, a smiling baby, a smiling black man, a smiling white man, a serious black man, a smiling white man wearing a hat, a smiling black man wearing a hat, a man and a woman.

PROCEDURE: Discuss the pictures with the child. Have him guess which one doesn't belong with the others. Ask him why it doesn't belong. Once the cat is removed, many choices are possible. Continue with different ways to eliminate the pictures.

Feel a Numeral

SUBJECT: Mathematics/Numerals

LEVEL: 5 years old

PURPOSE: Develop numeral recognition
Numerals one to ten

MATERIALS: None

PROCEDURE: "Write" a numeral on the child's back with your finger. Ask the child to name the numeral you wrote.

VARIATION: Challenge the child with numerals above ten.

Left (or Right) Day

SUBJECT: Mathematics/Ordering

LEVEL: 5 years old

PURPOSE: Introduce the concepts of left and right

MATERIALS: Decals, ribbon bracelets, or pipe-cleaner rings

PROCEDURE: After introducing the terms left and right, let today be "Left Day." Place the decal on the child's left hand (these will wash off but cannot be removed or transferred by the child). Reinforce throughout the day: raise your left hand, hop on your left foot, touch your left ear, etc. A few days later have a "Right Day."

Looby Loo

SUBJECT: Mathematics/Ordering

LEVEL: 5 years old

PURPOSE: Reinforce concepts of right and left

MATERIALS: None

PROCEDURE: While singing "Looby Loo," act out the directions:

> I put my right foot in,
> I put my right foot out,
> I give my right foot a
> shake, shake, shake
> And turn myself about.

Repeat for left foot and other parts of the body.

Personal–Social Skills (3–5 Years Old)

Let's Get in Control

SUBJECT: Personal–social skills/Language

LEVEL: 3 years old and up

PURPOSE: Practice self-control
             Develop listening skills
             Learn senses

MATERIALS: None

PROCEDURE: • Teach the child the following:

> Looking (touch your eyes)
> Listening (touch your ears)
> Quiet (index finger over lips)
> Sitting like an Indian (sit on floor with your legs crossed)
> With your hands on your lap (fold hands together and place them on your lap) (Fig. 14-2).

Tell the child that this is how she can get control. Anytime the child is not behaving appropriately, tell her to "get in control." Remind her that "control" is looking, listening, being quiet, and sitting like an "Indian" with hands on her lap.

Figure 14-2

- Utilize this as a way to get the child back on task and behaving appropriately. Have her remain in "getting in control" until she demonstrates that she is actually in control.
- Rule of thumb for time to stay in "getting in control" is 1 minute for each year old, e.g., 3 minutes for 3 years old. Never allow the child to resume an activity unless she is actually demonstrating appropriate behavior. If you allow your 3-year-old out after 3 minutes, but she is kicking and yelling, you will be reinforcing the negative behavior. React when she is demonstrating appropriate behavior even if it is less

than 3 minutes. The key is to reinforce positive behavior.

Please and Thank-You

SUBJECT: Personal–social skills

LEVEL: 4 years old and up

PURPOSE: Encourage child to say "please" with requests and "thank-you" for service or compliment

MATERIALS: A few of the child's favorite toys

PROCEDURE: Sit on the floor with the child directly across from you. Place some of her favorite toys between you. Ask the child, "May I please have the baby doll?" When the child hands you the baby doll, tell her "thank-you." Continue this with some of the other toys. Then have the child ask for the items by saying "please." Encourage the child to say "thank-you" when you give her the toy.

NOTE: Be a role model for the child. Be sure to say "please" with requests and "thank-you" with service and compliments. Children learn from what they see and hear.

Excuse Me

SUBJECT: Personal–social skills

LEVEL: 4 1/2 years old and up

PURPOSE: Encourage the child to say "excuse me" when interrupting or disturbing others

MATERIALS: None

PROCEDURE: Role-play situations such as bumping into the child. Say "excuse me" to the child. When you are talking to someone and the child keeps calling your attention, teach him to say "excuse me." When the child needs to walk in front of someone tell him to say "excuse me." Be a role model for the child. Observing your behavior will reinforce the appropriate time to say "excuse me."

Self-Help Skills (3–5 Years Old)

Buttons and Snaps

SUBJECT: Self-help skills

LEVEL: 3 years old and up

PURPOSE: Develop ability to unbutton front buttons and fasten large, front snaps
Develop fine motor ability

MATERIALS: Buttoning board, snap board (can be commercially bought in school supply stores or be made; see Figs. 10-59 and 10-60, pp. 145 and 146, respectively)
To make a buttoning board: Staple or nail a partial shirt front to a board. Sew on buttons beginning with very large ones on top and decrease in size as you go down. Be sure to cut button holes to fit each button.

PROCEDURE: • *Unbuttoning:* While the child is watching, unbutton all but one button. Ask the child to unbutton the last button. If it is necessary, partially unbutton each button and allow the child to finish the task. Allow her to start with the largest button first.
• *Snaps:* Demonstrate to the child how you fasten a snap. Be sure the child has enough strength to squeeze a snap together. If she has trouble, help her practice on other things that must be squeezed, e.g., pinch-type clothespins. Show the child how to position the top half of the snap over the bottom half, grasping the snap with fingers over one side and the thumb under the other, and squeezing it together.

Slowly snap all the snaps but one. Have your child do the last one. Next time, you do one and have the child do the rest. Assist the child as needed.

NOTE: Toy stores sell "Dress Me Dolls," which also aid in learning unbuttoning and fastening snaps (e.g., Ernie, Mickey Mouse). See Figs. 10-59 to 10-61(pp. 145–147), for pictures of materials.

APPENDIXES

Appendix 1

Basic Equipment and Supplies

STOP! Don't throw away those meat trays, empty toilet paper rolls, egg cartons, and much, much more. There are so many creative things you can do with "junk." The lists that follow will give you an idea of things to hold onto and utilize for activities with your child. You'll find many uses for these items as you read through the activities in this book.

There are also various kinds of equipment and supplies that may be utilized for activities involving creative exploration (art and music), fine motor skills (manipulatives), and language development (language and dramatic play).

"Junk Box"

Egg cartons
Milk cartons, jugs, and lids
Styrofoam meat trays
Cardboard fruit trays
Orange juice cans
Toilet paper rolls
Paper towel rolls
Empty spice bottles

Colorful junk mail
Old greeting cards
Small boxes (matches, spices, jello)
Plastic bottle caps
Yogurt container and lids
Margarine container and lids
Newspaper

255

Magazines
Film containers
Styrofoam chips/packing pieces
Fabric scraps
Yarn
Used computer paper
Large cartons/boxes
Clothespins
Wallpaper samples

Straws
Nylon stockings
Shoeboxes
Coat hanger
Oatmeal boxes
Small plastic medicine cups
Leggs' pantyhose eggs
Strawberry baskets
Paperbags

Art

Tempera paint
Paintbrushes
Play dough: make your own (recipe
    given on p. 60)
Magic markers
Crayons
Paper of assorted sizes and colors
Small bottles of glue
Rounded scissors
Felt pieces of various colors and
    sizes
Sponges of various shapes and sizes

Straws
Popsicle sticks
Feathers
Cottonballs
Construction paper in various
    colors (save scraps, too)
Shaving cream
Food coloring
Ivory Snow
Cookie cutters
Beans
String

Manipulatives

Sewing cards
Beads and string
Pegboards
Blocks (Attribute and kindergarten)
Small construction equipment
Molding materials

Visual Discrimination

Dominoes (pictures, shapes, numbers, colors)
Color games
Card games
Lotto games
Shape sorters

Dramatic Play

Wooden or cardboard stand for store, house, etc.
Dress-up clothes
Carriage
Shopping cart
Cash register
Dolls

Music

Records (see suggested list in Appendix 3)
Record player
Cassette player
Cassettes
Simple instruments: sticks, tambourine, bongos, maracas, chimes, bell,
    etc.

Language

Children's books (see suggested list in Appendix 2)
Puppets
Flannel board
Flannel shapes and pieces

Appendix 2

Suggested Preschool Literature

When sharing books with your child, you may simply talk about the pictures with her, read the text out loud, or make up your own story to go with the pictures. Choose books that you enjoy and don't be afraid to dramatize. If your child loses interest, feel free to choose another book or move to another activity.

Important things to keep in mind:

1. It is helpful to your child to be familiar with the story before reading it.
2. Make introductory remarks to get your child's interest. Comment on the cover, picture, title, colors on the cover, etc.
3. Start the story when your child is ready to listen.
4. Hold the book so that your child can see the pictures.
5. Show interest in and enthusiasm for books.
6. At the first sign of fatigue, finish the story quickly.

The following is a list of wonderful children's books that you may want to add to your child's collection. Many of these books have won awards for the story and/or illustrations. Some of the awards that have been presented are Caldecott Honor Book, Caldecott Medal, and New York Times Best Illustrated Book.

Action

Lerner, Sharon, and Mathieu, Joe. *Big Bird Says . . . A Game to Read and Play.*
New York: Random House/Children's Television Workshop, 1985.

Adventure

de Brunhoff, Jean. *The Story of Babar.* New York: Random House, 1933. Story
book.

Flack, Marjorie, and Wiese, Kurt. *The Story about Ping.* New York: Viking
Penguin/Puffin, 1933. Story book.

Van Allsburg, Chris. *The Garden of Abdul Gasazi.* New York: Houghton Mifflin,
1979. Story book (Caldecott Honor Book; New York Times Best Illustrated Book).

Animals

Brown, Marcia. *Once a Mouse . . .* New York: Macmillan/Aladdin, 1961. Picture book (Caldecott Medal; New York Times Best Illustrated Book).

Carle, Eric. *The Mixed-Up Chameleon.* New York: Crowell/Harper & Row,
1975. Picture book.

Langstaff, John. *Frog Went A-Courtin'.* New York: Harcourt Brace Jovanovich,
1955. Picture book (Caldecott Medal).

Lionni, Leo. *Frederick.* New York: William Morrow/Knopf, 1967. Picture book
(Caldecott Honor Book; New York Times Best Illustrated Book).

Lionni, Leo. *Swimmy.* New York: Random House/Knopf, 1963. Picture book
(Caldecott Honor Book; New York Times Best Illustrated Book).

Zolotow, Charlotte, and Sendak, Maurice. *Mr. Rabbit and the Lovely Present.*
New York: Harper & Row, 1962. Picture book (Caldecott Honor Book).

Baby's Books

Edwards, Annette, and Beach, Pearl. *Baby's First Book.* Los Angeles: Price Stern
Sloan, 1953. Picture book.

Kunhardt, Dorothy. *Pat the Bunny*. New York: Golden Books/Western, 1940. Picture book.

Ricklen, Neil. Super Chubby Books (A Little Simon Book): *Baby's Clothes; Baby's Toys; Baby's Friends; Baby's Home; Daddy and Me; Mommy and Me; Grandpa and Me; Grandma and Me*. New York: Simon & Schuster.

Wilburn, Kathlene. The Pudgy Board Book Series: *Pudgy Pals; The Pudgy Book of Babies; The Pudgy Book of Farm Animals; The Pudgy Book of Here We Go; The Pudgy Book of Make Believe; The Pudgy Book of Mother Goose; The Pudgy Book Toys; The Pudgy Bunny Book; The Pudgy Pat-A-Cake Book; The Pudgy Peek-A-Boo Book; The Pudgy I Love You Book; The Pudgy Noisy Book; The Little Engine that Could™ Pudgy Word Book*. New York: Grosset & Dunlap, Putnam Publishing Group.

Bedtime

Baird, Anne, and Fernandes, Eugenie. *Ride Away*. A Little Simon Book. New York: Simon & Schuster, 1987. Picture book.

Bang, Molly. *Ten, Nine, Eight*. New York: Morrow/Puffin, 1983. Picture book (Caldecott Honor Book).

Brown, Margaret Wise, and Hurd, Clement. *Goodnight Moon*. New York: Harper & Row, 1947. Picture book.

Morris, Ann, and Falconer, Elizabeth. *Quiet Night*. A Little Simon Book. New York: Simon & Schuster, 1986.

Ross, Katharine, and McCue, Lisa. *Nighty-Night Little One*. New York: Random House, 1988.

Family Matters

Munsch, Robert, and McGraw, Sheila. *Love You Forever*. Willowdale, Ontario, Canada: Firefly Books, 1986. Story book. Originally written in 1945.

Rylant, Cynthia, and Gammell, Stephen. *The Relatives Came*. Bradbury, 1985. Picture book. (Caldecott Honor Book; New York Times Best Illustrated Book).

Viorst, Judith, and Cruz, Ray. *Alexander and the Terrible, Horrible, No Good, Very Bad Day*. New York: Atheneum/Aladdin, 1972. Story book.

Yolen, Jane, and Schoenherr, John. *Owl Moon*. New York: Scholastic, Inc., 1987. Story book (Caldecott Medal).

Fantasy

MacDonald, Golden, and Weisgard, Leonard. *The Little Island*. New York: Doubleday Scholastic, 1946. Picture book (Caldecott Medal).
Sendak, Maurice. *Where the Wild Things Are*. New York: Harper & Row, 1962. Picture book (Caldecott Medal; New York Times Best Illustrated Book).

Folktale

Andersen, Hans Christian, and Van Nutt, Robert. *The Ugly Duckling*. New York: Knopf, 1986. Story book (New York Times Best Illustrated Book).
Blegvad, Erik. *The Three Little Pigs*. New York: Macmillan/Aladdin, 1980. Picture book.
Brown, Marcia. *Stone Soup*. New York: Macmillan/Aladdin, 1947. Picture book (Caldecott Honor Book).
Cauley, Lorinda Bryan. *The Town Mouse and the Country Mouse*. New York: Putnam, 1984. Story book.
Galdone, Paul. *The Three Billy Goats Gruff*. New York: Clarion Books, 1973. Picture book.
Hogrogian, Nonny. *One Fine Day*. New York: Macmillan/Aladdin, 1971. Picture book (Caldecott Medal).

Growing Up

Jonas, Ann. *When You Were a Baby*. New York: Morrow, 1982. Picture book.
Piper, Watty, Hauman, George, and Hauman, Doris. *The Little Engine That Could*. New York: Platt & Munk, 1930. Picture book.
Ross, Katharine, and Dunn, Phoebe. *When You Were a Baby*. New York: Learning Ladders/Random House, 1988. Picture book.
Silverstein, Shel. *The Giving Tree*. New York: Harper & Row, 1964. Story book.

History

Turkle, Brinton. *Thy Friend Obadiah*. New York: Viking Penguin/Puffin, 1969. Picture book (Caldecott Honor Book).

Holiday

Milhous, Katherine. *The Egg Tree*. New York: Macmillan/Aladdin, 1950. Picture book (Caldecott Medal).

Humor

Leaf, Munro, and Lawson, Robert. *The Story of Ferdinand*. New York: Viking Penguin/Puffin, 1936. Picture book (Caldecott Honor Book).

Low, Joseph. *Mice Twice*. New York: Macmillan, 1980. Picture book (Caldecott Honor Book).

Mordvinoff, Will, and Mordvinoff, Nicholas. *Finders Keepers*. New York: Harcourt Brace Jovanovich/Voyager/HBJ, 1951. Picture book (Caldecott Medal).

Rey, H. A. *Curious George*. New York: Doubleday, 1941. Picture book.

Rey, H. A. *Curious George Gets a Medal*. New York: Doubleday. Picture book.

Rey, H. A. *Curious George Rides a Bike*. New York: Doubleday. Picture book.

Manners

Joslin, Sesyle, and Sendak, Maurice. *What Do You Say, Dear?/What Do You Do, Dear?* New York: Harper & Row, 1958. Picture book (Caldecott Honor Book; New York Times Best Illustrated Book).

Multicultural

Aardema, Verna, and Vidal, Beatriz. *Bringing the Rain to Kapiti Plain*. New York: Scholastic, 1981.

Bishop Clair Huchet, and Wiese, Kurt. *The Five Chinese Brothers*. New York: Coward-McCann, 1938.

Feelings, Muriel, and Feelings, Tom. *Jambo Means Hello: Swahili Alphabet Book*. New York: Dial Books for Young Readers, 1974. Picture book (Caldecott Honor Book).

Freeman, Don. *Corduroy*. New York: Viking Penguin/Puffin, 1968. Picture book.

Freeman, Don. *A Pocket for Corduroy.* New York: Viking Penguin, 1978. Picture book.

Handforth, Thomas. *Mei Li.* New York: Doubleday, 1938 (the illustrations by the author were specially reproduced on copper plates).

Kimmel, Eric, and Hyman, Trina Schart. *Hershel and the Hanukkah Goblins.* New York: Scholastic, 1985 (1990 Caldecott Honor Book).

Simon, Norma, and Lasker, Joe. *All Kinds of Families.* Niles, Ill.: Albert Whitman & Company, 1976.

Simon, Norma, and Leder, Dora. *Why Am I Different?* Niles, Ill.: Albert Whitman & Company, 1976.

Surat, Michele Maria, and Mai, Vo-Dinh. *Angel Child, Dragon Child.* New York: Scholastic, 1983.

Yagawa, Sumiklo, and Akaba, Suekichi. Translated from the Japanese by Katherine Paterson. *The Crane Wife.* New York: Morrow, 1981 (New York Times Best Illustrated Book).

Young, Ed. *Lon Po Po.* New York: Scholastic, 1989. A Red-Riding Hood story from China (1990 Caldecott Honor Book).

Nature

Carle, Eric. *The Very Busy Spider.* New York: Scholastic, 1985. Picture book.

Carle, Eric. *The Very Hungry Caterpillar.* New York: Scholastic, 1969. Picture book.

Udry, Janice May, and Simont, Marc. *A Tree Is Nice.* New York: Harper & Row, 1956. Picture book (Caldecott Medal).

Potty Training

Rogers, Fred, and Judkis, Jim. *Going to the Potty.* New York: Putnam, 1986. Picture book.

Appendix 3

Suggested Preschool Recordings

Music can be related to many things such as special weather conditions (rainfall, snow, etc.), certain seasonal or holiday observances, or special topics. Whatever the situation, combining musical experiences with part of your daily routine and activities with your child demonstrates that music is something to be enjoyed as an integral part of life rather than as a separate entity. Music contributes in many ways to the growth and development of individuals.

Appropriate recordings of good quality should be available for use with your child. Such recordings can benefit your child in several ways: (1) they can be listened to for pure enjoyment; (2) they can be used as a guide for marching, dancing, or singing activities; and (3) they can be used to teach basic concepts.

Here is a list of suggested recordings. You may find many of these in your local school supply stores or contact the distributors listed for prices and delivery.

Ella Jenkins
Folkways Records & Service Corporation
43 W. 61st Street
New York, NY

Jambo and Other Call-and-Response Songs and Chants (1974)
"Voices in Training" (for the Chicago Children's Choir)
Order Number FC 7661

You'll Sing a Song and I'll Sing a Song (1966)
With members of the Urban Gateways Children's Chorus
Order Number FC 7664

Ella Jenkins
Scholastic Records
906 Sylvan Avenue
Englewood Cliffs, NJ 07632

Counting Games and Rhythms for the Little Ones (1965)
With children from Lake Meadows Nursery School
Order Number SC 7679

Kimbo Educational
P.O. Box 477
Long Branch, NJ 07740

Georgiana Liccione Stewart: *Fun Activities* (1973)
Order Number KIM 9076

Georgiana Stewart: *Preschool Aerobic Fun* (1983)
Order Number KIM 7052

Raffi: *More Singable Songs* (1977)
With Ken Whiteley
Order Number SL-004

Raffi: *Singable Songs for the Very Young* (1976)
With Ken Whiteley
Order Number SL-002

Melody House Publishing Co.
819 N.W. 92nd
Oklahoma City, OK 73114

Adventures in Sound
Order Number MH-55

Fables in Action
Order Number MH-21

Pre-School Fitness
Order Number MH-61

Rhythm and Rhyme
Activities for early childhood
Body movement, hand and finger play
Order Number MH-87

Steve Millang and Greg Scelsa
Youngheart Records
Los Angeles, CA 90027

Kidding Around with Greg and Steve (1985)
Educate, motivate, enrich, entertain—for ages 3 to 8
Order Number VR 007R

On the Move with Greg and Steve (1983)
Activity songs, rhythm and movement, creative play, sing-alongs
Order Number VR 005R

Quiet Moments with Greg and Steve (1983)
Quiet activities, resting music
Order Number VR 006R

We All Live Together, Vol. 1 (1975)
Rhythm and movement, activity songs, call and response, sing-alongs,
    resting songs
Order Number VR 001R

We All Live Together, Vol. 3 (1979)
Basic skills, rhythm and movement, sing-alongs, call and response, cre-
    ative play, resting
Order Number VR 003R

We All Live Together, Vol. 4 (1980)
Basic skills, rhythm and movement, sing-alongs, call and response, cre-
    ative play, resting
Order Number VR 004R

Hap Palmer
Educational Activities, Inc.
Box 392
Freeport, NY 11520

> *Creative Movement and Rhythmic Expression* (1971)
> Order Number AR 533

> *The Feel of Music* (1974)
> Order Number AR 556

> *Feelin' Free* (1976)
> A personalized approach to vocabulary and language development
> Order Number AR 517

> *Getting to Know Myself* (1972)
> Order Number AR 543

> *Holiday Songs and Rhythms* (1980)
> Order Number AR 538

> *Homemade Band* (1973)
> Order Number AR 545

> *Learning Basic Skills through Music* (1969)
> Vocabulary
> Order Number AR 521

> *Learning Basic Skills through Music,* Vol. I (1969)
> Order Number AR 514

> *Learning Basic Skills through Music,* Vol. II (1969)
> Order Number AR 522

> *Learning Basic Skills through Music,* Vol. III (1970)
> Health and safety
> Order Number AR 526

> *Math Readiness: Addition and Subtraction* (1972)
> Order Number AR 541

> *Math Readiness: Vocabulary and Concepts* (1972)
> Order Number AR 540

Mod Marches (1980)
Order Number AR 527

Modern Tunes for Rhythms and Instruments (1969)
Order Number AR 523

Movin' (1973)
Order Number AR 546

Pretend (1975)
Order Number AR 563

Peter Pan Records
Newark, NJ

Beryl Berney: *I'd Like to Teach the World to Sing*

Lois and Bram Sharon
Elephant Records
P.O. Box 101, Station Z
Toronto, Canada M5N 2Z3

In the Schoolyard (1981)
20-page illustrated booklet with words, music, games, and actions

Mainly Mother Goose (1984)
Songs and rhymes for merry young souls

One Elephant, Deux Elephants (1978)
A children's record for the whole family

Appendix 4

Suggested Preschool Videos

Television and videos can benefit children if not overused and if the programs are selected carefully. Here is a list of videos that you may find useful and of interest to supplement the hands-on activities in Part II. Many of these videos may be found in your local video, department, and discount stores. If not, contact the distributors listed for prices and availability.

Hanna Anderson
Northwest Videoworks, Inc.
1631 S.W. Columbia
Portland, OR 97201
503-227-7202

Hanna: The Video

Charlotte's Web (1972)
Hanna-Barbera-Sagittarius Production
Paramount Pictures
5555 Melrose Avenue
Hollywood, CA 90038

Walt Disney Series
Buena Vista Home Video
Burbank, CA 91521

   Sing-along songs:

      Vol. 1: Heigh-Ho
      Vol. 2: Zip-a-Dee-Doo-Dah
      Vol. 3: You Can Fly
      Vol. 4: The Bare Necessities
      Vol. 5: Fun with Music
      Vol. 6: Under the Sea

Golden Books Collection
Western Publishing Company, Inc.
Racine, Wisconsin 53404

National Association for the Education of Young Children (NAEYC)
1834 Connecticut Avenue, N.W.
Washington, D.C. 20009
1-800-424-2460
   Ask for catalog. Many wonderful tapes for children, parents, educators, and caregivers.

Sesame Street Collection
Children's Television Workshop
Random House Home Video

Dr. Seuss Collection
Random House Home Video

Wee Sing
Price Stern Sloan, Inc.

         King Cole's Party (1987)
         A merry musical celebration

Suggested Preschool Software

In addition to using your home computer for your personal and business needs, your preschooler can also use it as a reinforcement to those interesting hands-on activities in Part II. Contact the publisher for computer requirements and prices. Here is just a small sampling to get you started.

Hartley Courseware, Inc.
P.O. Box 419
Dimondale, MI 48821
1-800-247-1380

Colors and Shapes. Helps children discriminate colors, match shapes, and use familiar shapes to reproduce a model.

Observation and Classification. Helps children sharpen their observational skills and classify familiar objects by use and function.

Conservation and Counting. Helps children focus on one-to-one correspondence, conservation of numbers, and matching sets.

Size and Logic. Helps children improve the ability to discriminate among objects according to size.

Ollie and Seymour. Children practice directionality, thinking skills, and traffic safety in a simulated community park.

DLM
P.O. Box 4000
One DLM Park
Allen, TX 75002
1-800-527-4747

> *Curious George in Outer Space.* Children learn comparison concepts:
> tall/taller/tallest, long/longer/longest, etc.

> *Curious George Visits the Library.* Children learn pointer words and
> concepts: in/out, up/down, on top of/in front of, etc.

Optimum Resources, Inc.
10 Station Place
Norfolk, CT 06058
1-800-327-1473

> *Stickybear Numbers.* Reinforces number and counting skills.

> *Stickybear Opposites.* Encourages a thorough understanding of op-
> posites.

References

Chapter 1

1. Ellen Galinsky, "Raising Children in the 1990's: The Challenges for Parents, Educators, and Business," *Young Children* 45 (January 1990), pp. 2–3.

Chapter 2

1. Herbert Ginsburg and Sylvia Opper, *Piaget's Theory of Intellectual Development: An Introduction* (Englewood Cliffs, NJ: Prentice-Hall, 1969), p. 62.
2. Mary Ann Spencer Pulaski, *Your Baby's Mind and How It Grows: Piaget's Theory for Parents* (New York: Harper & Row, 1978), p. 15.
3. Ibid, p. 31.
4. Ibid, p. 48.
5. Jean Piaget, *Origins of Intelligence in Children* (New York: Norton, 1963), p. 215.
6. Pulaski, *Baby's Mind,* p. 87.
7. Jean Piaget and Barbel Inhelder, *The Psychology of the Child* (New York: Basic Books, 1969), pp. 11–12.

Chapter 3

1. Jean Piaget, *Six Psychological Studies* (New York: Random House, 1967), p. 18.

2. Herbert Ginsburg and Sylvia Opper, *Piaget's Theory of Intellectual Development: An Introduction* (Englewood Cliffs, NJ: Prentice-Hall, 1969), p. 84.
3. B. Wadsworth, *Piaget's Theory of Cognitive Development* (New York: Longman, 1971), p. 76.
4. Mary Ann Spencer Pulaski, *Understanding Piaget* (New York: Harper & Row, Publishers, 1979), p. 43.

Chapter 4

1. B. Wadsworth, *Piaget's Theory of Development* (New York: Longman, 1971), p. 18.
2. B. Gruen, "Experiences Affecting the Development of Number Conservations in Children," *Child Development* 36 (1965), pp. 964–979.

Chapter 5

1. Jean Piaget, *Six Psychological Studies* (New York: Random House, 1968), p. 11.
2. Jean Piaget and Barbel Inhelder, *The Psychology of the Child* (New York: Basic Books, 1969), p. 505.
3. Anthony C. Maffei and Patricia Buckley, *Teaching Preschool Math: Foundations and Activities* (New York: Human Sciences Press/Plenum, 1980), p. 22.
4. H. Gruber and J. Voneche, eds., *Essential Piaget* (New York: Basic Books, 1977), p. 71.
5. Ibid, p. 72.
6. Ibid, p. 75.
7. Ibid, p. 70.
8. Ibid, p. 163.

Chapter 6

1. H. Gruber and J. Voneche, eds., *Essential Piaget* (New York: Basic Books, 1977), p. 371.
2. Richard Copeland, *How Children Learn Mathematics: Teaching Implications of Piaget's Research* (New York: Macmillan, 1979), p. 90

3. Gruber and Voneche, *Essential Piaget,* p. 313.
4. Ibid, p. 315.
5. Ibid, p. 317.

Chapter 7

1. Anthony C. Maffei and Patricia Buckley, *Teaching Preschool Math: Foundations and Activities* (New York: Human Sciences Press/Plenum, 1980), p. 150.
2. H. Gruber and J. Voneche, eds., *Essential Piaget* (New York: Basic Books, 1977), p. 586.
3. Ibid, p. 589.
4. Ibid, p. 593.
5. Ibid.
6. Pulaski, *Piaget,* p. 165.
7. Gruber and Voneche, *Essential Piaget,* p. 260.
8. Ibid, p. 264.
9. Ibid, p. 566.
10. Ibid, p. 568
11. Mary Ann Spencer Pulaski, *Understanding Piaget* (New York: Harper & Row, 1979), p. 178.

Chapter 8

1. T. Berry Brazelton, *Working and Caring* (Reading, MA: Addison-Wesley, 1987), p. 143.

Bibliography

Part I

Beck, K. Piaget does not live on "Sesame Street." *Educational Technology,* 1977, 53, 610–619.

Burton, G. Helping parents help their preschool children. *Arithmetic Teacher,* May, 1978, 12–14.

Copeland, R. *How Children Learn Mathematics: Teaching Implications of Piaget's Research.* New York: Macmillan, 1979.

Elkind, D. Early childhood education: A Piagetian perspective. *National Elementary Principal,* 1971, 51, 48–55.

Flavell, J. *The Developmental Psychology of Jean Piaget.* Princeton, NJ: D. Van Nostrand, 1963.

Furth, H. G. *Piaget for Teachers.* Englewood Cliffs, NJ: Prentice-Hall, 1969.

Furth, H., and Wachs, H. *Piaget's Theory in Practice: Thinking Goes to School.* New York: Oxford University Press, 1974.

Galloway, C. *Psychology for Learning and Teaching.* New York: McGraw-Hill, 1976.

Ginsburg, H., and Opper, S. *Piaget's Theory of Intellectual Development: An Introduction.* Englewood Cliffs, NJ: Prentice-Hall, 1969.

Gruber, H., and Voneche, J. (Eds.). *Essential Piaget.* New York: Basic Books, 1977. This is an excellent resource text containing the central excerpts from many of Piaget's writings. The editors provide informative summaries before each excerpt.

Gruen, G. E. Experiences affecting the development of number conservations in children. *Child Development,* 1965, 36, 964–979.

Levenson, D. Whatever happened to early chilldhood education? *Instructor,* October, 1977, 84(3) 67, 72, 134, 135, 138.

Piaget, J. How children form mathematical concepts. *Scientific American,* November, 1953.

Piaget, J. *Six Psychological Studies* (D. Elkind, Ed.). New York: Random House, 1968.

Piaget, J., and Inhelder, B. *The Psychology of the Child.* New York: Basic Books, 1969.

Piaget, J. *Science of Education and the Psychology of the child.* New York: Orion, 1970.

Rea, R., and Reys, R. Mathematical competencies of entering kindergarteners. *Arithmetic Teacher,* January, 1970, 17, 65–74.

Sigel, E., and Hooper, F. *Logical Thinking in Children: Research Based on Piaget's Theory.* New York: Holt, Rinehart, and Winston, 1968.

Wadsworth, B. *Piaget for the Classroom Teacher.* New York: Longman, 1978.

Wadsworth, B. *Piaget's Theory of Cognitive Development.* New York: Longman, 1971.

Woods, R. Preschool arithmetic is important. *Arithmetic Teacher,* January, 1968, 15, 7–9.

Part II

Bredekamp, S. (Ed.). National Association for the Education for Young Children. *Developmentally Appropriate Practice in Early Childhood Programs Serving Children from Birth through Age 8.* Washington, D.C.: National Association for the Education of Young Children, 1987.

Kiester, E., Jr., and Kiester, S. V., and Editors of *Better Homes and Gardens. New Baby Book.* Des Moines, IA: Meredith Corporation, 1985.

Maffei, A. C., and Buckley, P. *Teaching Preschool Math: Foundations and Activities.* New York: Plenum/Human Sciences Press, 1980.

Magee, P. M., and Ornstein, M. R. *Come with Us to Play Group: A Handbook for Parents and Teachers of Young Children.* Englewood Cliffs, NJ: Prentice-Hall, 1981.

Sanford, A. R., and Zelman, J. G. *Learning Accomplishment Profile,* Chapel Hill Training-Outreach Project. Winston-Salem, NC: Kaplan Press, 1981.

Sawyers, J. K., and Rogers, C. S. *Helping Young Children Develop through Play: A Practical Guide for Parents, Caregivers, and Teachers.* Washington, D.C.: National Association for the Education for Young Children, 1988.

Suggested Readings

Blansett, M. L. *Put a Frog in Your Pocket! Educational Art Activities for Young Children.* Nashville, TN: Incentive Publications, 1985.

Chubet, C. *Play and Learn: Social and Mental Growth in the First Two Years.* CT: Longmeadow Press, 1988.

Eden, A. N. *Positive Parenting: How to Raise a Healthier and Happier Child (from Birth to Three Years).* New York: Alvin N. Eden, M.D., by arrangement with Macmillan, 1980.

Gates, F. *Easy to Make Puppets.* Englewood Cliffs, NJ: Prentice-Hall, 1976.

Haselden, M., and Pass, G. *Teddy's Book: A Ladybird Play and Learn Activity Book (Ages 3 to 6).* Auburn, ME: Ladybird Books, 1989.

Jenkins, K.S. *Kinder-Krunchies: Healthy Snack Recipes for Children.* Pleasant Hill, CA: Discovery Toys.

Keister, E., Jr., and Kiester, S. V., and Editors of *Better Homes and Gardens Books. Your Baby Grows Up: 18 Months to 6 Years.* Des Moines, IA: Meredith Corporation, 1987.

Lehane, S. *The Creative Child: How to Encourage the Natural Creativity of Your Preschooler.* Englewood Cliffs, NJ: Prentice-Hall, 1979.

Link, M. *Outdoor Education: A Manual for Teaching in Nature's Classroom.* Englewood Cliffs, NJ: Prentice-Hall, 1981.

Miller, K. *Ages and Stages: Developmental Descriptions and Activities, Birth through Eight Years.* Marshfield, MA: Telshare Publishing Company, 1985.

Olney, R. R., and Olney, P. *Easy to Make Magic.* Englewood Cliffs, NJ: Prentice-Hall, 1979.

Rountree, B., Shuptrine, M. B., Gordon, J. F., and Taylor, N. Y. *Creative Teaching with Puppets.* University: University of Alabama Press, 1981.

Sullivan, M. *Feeling Strong, Feeling Free: Movement Exploration for Young Children.* Washington, D.C.: National Association for the Education of Young Children, 1982.

Index